THE STRANGE CAREER OF
JIM CROW

THE STRANGE CAREER OF
JIM CROW

C. Vann Woodward

A Galaxy Book

New York
Oxford University Press

TO

Charlottesville
and the hill that
looks down upon her,
Monticello

Preface

THE PERIOD OF HISTORY that gave rise to the laws of segregation, which we call the 'Jim Crow' system, is still wrapped in a good deal of obscurity. For all but the elderly it lies below the threshold of living memory. Yet it is too recent to have received serious investigation from any but a few specialists. Their findings have not made their way into the books read by intelligent laymen, much less into the popular mind.

Southerners and other Americans of middle age or even older are contemporaries of Jim Crow. They grew up along with the system. Unable to remember a time when segregation was not the general rule and practice, they have naturally assumed that things have 'always been that way.' Or if not always, then 'since slavery times,' or 'since The War,' or 'since

Reconstruction.' Some even think of the system as existing along with slavery. Few have any idea of the relative recency of the Jim Crow laws, or any clear notion of how, when, and why the system arose. There is nothing in their history books that gives them much help. And there is considerable in the books that is likely to mislead and confuse them.

It has been my experience that impatient reformers are as surprised or incredulous as foot-dragging conservatives when confronted by some of the little-known history of Jim Crow. The fact seems to be that people of all shades of opinion — radical, liberal, conservative, and reactionary — as well as people of both the Negro and white races have often based their opinions on shaky historical foundations or downright misinformation. Some of the most direful predictions of disaster as well as some of the most hopeful forecasts of interracial felicity have been so founded. And so also have some recent programs of reform as well as strategems of resistance to reform.

The twilight zone that lies between living memory and written history is one of the favorite breeding places of mythology. This particular twilight zone has been especially prolific in the breeding of legend. The process has been aided by the old prejudices, the deeply stirred emotions, and the sectional animosities that always distort history in any zone, however well illuminated by memory or research.

viii

The distortions and perversions that have taken place in Jim Crow history are all the more regrettable in view of the current debate that rages over segregation. The national discussion over the questions of how deeply rooted, how ineradicable, and how amenable to change the segregation practices really are is being conducted against a background of faulty or inadequate historical information. And some of the most widely held sociological theories regarding segregation are based upon erroneous history.

It is my hope in these pages to turn a few beams of light into the twilight zone and if possible to light up a few of its corners. A general illumination will have to wait upon more research and investigation — work that very much needs doing. I also make the attempt to relate the origins and development of Jim Crowism to the bewilderingly rapid changes that have occurred in race relations during the past few years. Since I am therefore dealing with a period of the past that has not been adequately investigated, and also with events of the present that have come too rapidly and recently to have been properly digested and understood, it is rather inevitable that I shall make some mistakes. I shall expect and hope to be corrected. In the meantime, I feel that the need of the times for whatever light the historian has to shed upon a perplexing and urgent problem justifies this somewhat premature effort.

I wish to acknowledge my obligations to the work of other investigators mentioned in the 'Suggested Reading' at the end of the book. I am particularly indebted to the monographs of Professors George B. Tindall and Vernon L. Wharton. Four generous and obliging friends have read and criticized the manuscript. They are Professor Howard K. Beale of the University of Wisconsin, Professor Manning J. Dauer of the University of Florida, Professor John Hope Franklin of Brooklyn College, and Professor Rupert B. Vance of the University of North Carolina. I have profited greatly from their suggestions.

These lectures were delivered early in the fall at the University of Virginia as the James W. Richard Lectures of 1954. They were given before unsegregated audiences and they were received in that spirit of tolerance and open-mindedness that one has a right to expect at a university with such a tradition and such a founder.

C. V. W.

The Queen's College
Oxford
February 1955

Foreword to the Galaxy Edition

IN THE ORIGINAL EDITION of this book, deliberate emphasis was placed upon the relative recency of the growth and development of the segregation pattern in race relations. Another emphasis, dictated in part by limitations of space, was placed upon the South as the central theater for this historic development. Both the emphasis upon time and upon place would still seem to be justified. But emphasis, however justified, sometimes comes at a cost to things not emphasized. The new edition of this book provides a welcome opportunity to treat of some of those things and to clarify points that the original edition left unclear.

In the first place, although the segregation system is relatively new, it is grounded upon theories and attitudes that are not at all new. It is a mis-

take to assume that the ideas of innate Negro inferiority and white supremacy originated along
with the Jim Crow system, for they are much
older. Segregation is, after all, only the latest phase
in the long history of the white man's ways of fixing the Negro's status, his 'place.' There have been
other and harsher phases, including bondage and
limited servitude. Slavery, peonage, and abortive
types of apprenticeship have had their day. Exploitation of the Negro by the white man goes
back to the beginning of relations between the
races, and so do race conflict, brutality, and injustice. Along with these practices, and in justification and defense of them, there developed the old
assumptions of Anglo-Saxon superiority and African inferiority, white supremacy and Negro subordination. In so far as segregation is based upon
these assumptions, therefore, it is based upon the
old proslavery argument and has remote roots in
the slavery period.

Slavery provided more than ideological roots
for segregation. It is true that there were many
aspects of plantation slavery that promoted intimacy between the races and rendered segregation
impracticable. The supervision, care, exploitation,
and policing of slaves necessitated many contacts
and accustomed the races in the South to a degree
of intimacy unequaled in other parts of the country, intimacy outlasting slavery itself. It is doubt-

xii

ful, however, that much of the personal association and contact extended beyond the household servants. This class, of course, constituted a relatively small proportion of the slaves. The great bulk of the slaves, the field hands, shared little but the harsher type of contact with white people. There is little in this record that supports the legend of racial harmony in slavery times.

In so far as the Negro's status was fixed and proclaimed by enslavement there was no need or occasion to resort to segregation to establish his caste and his subordination. But within the slavery regime itself there were Negroes whose status was not established by slavery. These were the several hundred thousand free, or quasi-free, Negroes. It was in the treatment accorded these people in both North and South that the ante-bellum period came nearest foreshadowing segregation. Denied full rights and privileges of citizens, deprived of equality in the courts, and restricted in their freedom of assembly and freedom of movements, the so-called free Negro shared many of the deprivations of the slave. In addition measures of ostracism were leveled at members of this class to emphasize their status.

Outside the South the free Negroes fared little better than they did in the slave states. They were often segregated in churches and placed in separate schools. The Jim Crow car was a feature of three

xiii

railroads in Massachusetts as late as 1843. Stage coach and steamboat lines as well as railroads, usually on their own initiative rather than by force of law, required the separation of the races in several states. Laws prohibiting intermarriage between Negroes and whites were common in both Northern and Southern states.

After the fall of the Confederacy many white people of the South, and some in the North as well, showed a strong disposition to regard the newly liberated freedmen in the same way they had the despised free Negro before the war and to subject them to the same treatment. One result was that railroads, steamboats, and other carriers in the South began to deny Negroes the use of first-class accommodations. Passenger trains of that period, even the better ones, commonly had only two coaches, one usually called the 'ladies' car,' to which white men who paid the price were also admitted, and the other the 'smoking car' or 'gentlemen's car.' They were in effect first and second-class accommodations. On the smaller railroads the second coach was likely to be an old car or even a freight car. Smoke, tobacco juice, and profanity did not increase the attractiveness of second-class travel. The great bulk of freedmen and the majority of whites could rarely afford first-class accommodations anyway, but those Negroes who could were regularly denied them.

In 1865 the Mississippi legislature gave the force of law to the practices already adopted by the railroads by forbidding 'any freedman, negro, or mulatto to ride in any first-class passenger cars, set apart, or used by and for white persons . . .' Exception was made of Negroes traveling with their mistresses as nurses. Nothing was said about the mixing of races in second-class cars, and there was no requirement that a car for the exclusive use of Negroes be provided. The Florida legislature went a step further the same year by forbidding whites to use accommodations set apart for exclusive use of Negroes, as well as excluding Negroes from cars reserved for whites. But the Florida law did not require the railroads to provide separate cars for either race, nor did it prohibit the mixing of races in the 'smoking cars.' Texas carried the development further in 1866 with a law that simply required all railroad companies to 'attach to passenger trains one car for the special accommodation of freedmen.'

These three elementary and abortive laws were on the books only a short time, for they were quickly repealed by the Reconstruction legislatures. The discriminatory practice of denying Negroes the use of first-class accommodations nevertheless continued to be the rule, with the exception of some railroads of the Seaboard South, throughout Reconstruction and into the period following, until the era of consistent, thorough, and legally sanctioned segregation.

A second candidate for the South's 'first Jim Crow law' is an act adopted by the legislature of Tennessee in 1881. This law required all railroad companies in the state to 'furnish separate cars, or portions of cars cut off by partitioned walls' in which Negro passengers who paid for first-class accommodations could have the same facilities enjoyed by whites who paid the same fare. The white members of the legislature, one house of which was controlled by the Republican party and contained four Negro members, regarded the measure as a concession to the Negroes and an improvement of their condition, and the Republican governor of the state signed the bill without hesitation. It is evident that many railroads of the state flouted the law of 1881 and continued their old practices. Those trains that did carry three or more passenger cars usually provided what was sometimes called the 'colored' first class car and at times the 'Jim Crow' car. Negroes with first-class tickets were assigned to it, but it was not exclusively for their use for it was also made available to white passengers. Segregation was therefore not achieved by the law, nor did it alter the situation in the second-class cars. Tennessee, like most of the Southern states, did not arrive at real

xvi

separation of the races in this field until the 'nineties.

It was never the intention of anything said in the following pages to suggest that the absence of segregation implied the acceptance of Negroes as social equals. Such acceptance by native whites of the South was as rare before the era of segregation as it was at the height of that era. Segregation certainly meant a further lowering of the Negro's status, but it did not imply a fall from full equality and social integration. The fact was that the race had never been accepted on those terms.

There is plenty of evidence to indicate that from the first the freedmen were often denied their civil rights and subjected to discrimination, exclusion, and mistreatment by railroads, hotels, inns, and places of entertainment generally. But it is also clear that the era of genuine segregation was yet to come — the era when the principle was consciously and deliberately applied to all possible areas of contact between the races, and when the code became a hard-and-fast dogma of the white race. What delayed the coming of that era, how it came and why, and what were its consequences are the questions with which this book proposes to deal.

Contents

THE STRANGE CAREER OF
JIM CROW

INTRODUCTION /

Of Reconstructions and the South

THE PEOPLE OF THE SOUTH should be the last Americans to expect indefinite continuity of their institutions and social arrangements. Other Americans have less reason to be prepared for sudden change and lost causes. Apart from Southerners, Americans have enjoyed a historical continuity that is unique among modern peoples. The stream of national history, flowing down from seventeenth-century sources, reached a fairly level plain in the eighteenth century. There it gathered mightily in volume and span from its tributaries, but it continued to flow like the Mississippi over an even bed between relatively level banks.

Southern history, on the other hand, took a different turn in the nineteenth century. At intervals the even bed gave way under the stream, which sometimes plunged over falls or swirled through rapids. These breaks in the course of Southern history go by the names of slavery and secession, independence and defeat, emancipation and reconstruction, redemption and reunion. Some are more precipitous and dramatic than others. Some result in sheer drops and falls, others in narrows and rapids. The distance between them, and thus the extent of smooth sailing and stability, varies a great deal.

Considerably the longest of the stretches of relative stability between major historic faults over which Southern history flows has been that since the break that goes under several names, among them Redemption,* or the Compromise of 1877. It will doubtless occur to some that in fixing upon this period as the longest I may have overlooked the 'Old South' — the South of the Cotton Kingdom and plantation slavery. But the Old South, so far as the Cotton Kingdom was concerned, was 'old' only by courtesy, or to distinguish it from a 'New South.' Purely on the ground of longevity the Old South did not really last long enough in the larger part of the region to deserve the name 'old.' And in some states it scarcely attained a respectable middle age.

---

* 'Redemption' refers to the overthrow of the carpetbaggers and their regime. 'Redeemers' refers to the Southern leaders who accomplished the overthrow.

By comparison with the Old South, the so-called New South, already well past the three-score-and-ten mark, is very old indeed.

Lacking the tradition of historical continuity possessed by their fellow countrymen, more familiar through experience with the shifting fortunes of history, Southerners have less reason to expect the indefinite duration of any set of social institutions. Their own history tells them of a well-established society whose institutions were buttressed by every authority of learning, law, and constitution, supported by the church, the schools, and the press, and cherished devotedly by the people. In spite of all this they know that this old order and its institutions perished quite completely. It was replaced by a new order that had behind it all the authority and confidence of a victorious North, a constitution newly revised by the victors, and the force of the national army. The social and political changes were inspired by a North that was in a revolutionary mood, determined to stop at nothing short of a complete and thoroughgoing reformation. Yet this new order disappeared even more swiftly than its predecessor and was in turn replaced by a third.

Each successive regime in the South had had its characteristic economic and industrial organization, its system of politics, and its social arrangements. It is difficult to assign priority of importance to any one aspect of a particular regime, for all aspects were parts of a whole and it is hard to imagine one without the other. The peculiarity most often used to distinguish one order from another, however, has been the relation between races, or more particularly the status of the Negro. This is not to contend that the Negro's status has been what one historian has called the 'central theme' or basic determinant of Southern history. There is in fact an impressive amount of evidence indicating that the Negro's status and changes therein have been the product of more impersonal forces. Such forces have been discovered at work behind the conflicts that resulted in the overthrow of slavery, the frustration of the Lincoln and Johnson plan of Restoration, the establishment of Radical Reconstruction, the overthrow of Reconstruction, and the foundation of the new order. In fixing upon the Negro's status and race relations, therefore, I am not advancing a theory of historical causation but adopting common usage in characterizing the successive phases of Southern history.

The phase that began in 1877 was inaugurated by the withdrawal of federal troops from the South, the abandonment of the Negro as a ward of the nation, the giving up of the attempt to guarantee the freedman his civil and political equality, and the acquiescence of the rest of the country in the South's demand that the whole problem be left to the disposition of the dominant Southern white people.

What the new status of the Negro would be was not at once apparent, nor were the Southern white people themselves so united on that subject at first as has been generally assumed. The determination of the Negro's 'place' took shape gradually under the influence of economic and political conflicts among divided white people — conflicts that were eventually resolved in part at the expense of the Negro. In the early years of the twentieth century, it was becoming clear that the Negro would be effectively disfranchised throughout the South, that he would be firmly relegated to the lower rungs of the economic ladder, and that neither equality nor aspirations for equality in any department of life were for him.

The public symbols and constant reminders of his inferior position were the segregation statutes, or 'Jim Crow' * laws. They constituted the most elaborate and formal expression of sovereign white opinion upon the subject. In bulk and detail as well as in effectiveness of enforcement the segregation codes were comparable with the black codes of the old regime, though the laxity that mitigated the

* The origin of the term 'Jim Crow' applied to Negroes is lost in obscurity. Thomas D. Rice wrote a song and dance called 'Jim Crow' in 1832, and the term had become an adjective by 1838. The first example of 'Jim Crow law' listed by the *Dictionary of American English* is dated 1904. But the expression was used by writers in the 1890's who are quoted on the following pages.

harshness of the black codes was replaced by a rigidity that was more typical of the segregation code. That code lent the sanction of law to a racial ostracism that extended to churches and schools, to housing and jobs, to eating and drinking. Whether by law or by custom, that ostracism eventually extended to virtually all forms of public transportation, to sports and recreations, to hospitals, orphanages, prisons, and asylums, and ultimately to funeral homes, morgues, and cemeteries.

The new Southern system was regarded as the 'final settlement,' the 'return to sanity,' the 'permanent system.' Few stopped to reflect that previous systems had also been regarded as final, sane, and permanent by their supporters. The illusion of permanency was encouraged by the complacency of a long-critical North, the propaganda of reconciliation, and the resigned compliance of the Negro. The illusion was strengthened further by the passage of several decades during which change was averted or minimized. Year after year spokesmen of the region assured themselves and the world at large that the South had taken its stand, that its position was immovable, that alteration was unthinkable, come what might. As late as 1928 Professor Ulrich B. Phillips described the South as 'a people with a common resolve indomitably maintained — that it shall be and remain a white man's country.' And that conviction, he observed, 'whether expressed with

8

the frenzy of a demagogue or maintained with a patrician's quietude, is the cardinal test of a Southerner and the central theme of Southern history.' Whether it was the 'central theme' or not, both demagogue and patrician continued to express it in varying degrees of frenzy or quietude. The professors called it 'the maintenance of Caucasian civilization' and the stump speakers called it 'white supremacy.' They were different ways of expressing the same determination and endorsing the same objective.

Yet in the face of apparent solidarity of Southern resistance to change, a resistance that continues to receive firm and eloquent expression in some quarters, it has become increasingly plain that another era of change is upon the South and that the changes achieved or demanded are in the very area traditionally held most inviolable to alteration. Not since the First Reconstruction has this area been invaded from so many quarters, with such impatience of established practice and such insistent demand for immediate reform. Beginning about two decades ago, but reaching full momentum only in the decade since the Second World War, the New Reconstruction shows no signs of having yet run its course or even of having slackened its pace.

It had not one but many sources. Perhaps the most conspicuous was the United States Supreme Court and its succession of dramatic decisions down to

1954. But in addition there were many others, including the pressure and propaganda organizations for civil rights — both Negro and white, Northern and Southern. There were also executive orders of Presidents, policy decisions of federal agencies, actions by labor unions, professional organizations, churches, corporation executives, and educational leaders. Perhaps the most unusual and at the same time most strikingly effective agencies of radical change were the officers of the army, navy, and air force, acting under orders of both Democratic and Republican administrations. The New Reconstruction, unlike the old, was not the monopoly of one of the great political parties. Behind these conscious and deliberate agencies of change were such great impersonal forces of history as lay behind emancipation, the First Reconstruction, and Redemption. They included economic revolution, rapid urbanization, and war — war in a somewhat new dimension, called total war.

The New Reconstruction addressed itself to all the aspects of racial relations that the first one attacked and even some that the First Reconstruction avoided or neglected. These included political, economic, and civil rights. Few sections of the segregation code have escaped attack, for the assault has been leveled at the Jim Crow system in trains, buses, and other common carriers; in housing and working conditions; in restaurants, theaters, and hospitals;

10

in playgrounds, public parks, swimming pools, and organized sports, to mention a few examples. Most recently the attack has been carried into two areas in which the First Reconstruction radicals made no serious effort: segregation in the armed services and in the public schools.

With no more perspective than we have as yet upon this New Reconstruction it would be rash to attempt any definitive assessment of its effectiveness, of the motives behind it, or of its importance and meaning in Southern history. It may well be that after a few generations the historians will conclude that, compared with the contemporaneous abandonment of the one-crop system, or the rapid pace of urbanization and of industrialization, the crumbling of the segregation system was of relatively minor historical significance.

What the perspective of years will lend to the meaning of change we cannot know. We can, however, recognize and define the area and extent of change. I shall even be so bold as to maintain that recent changes are of sufficient depth and impact as to define the end of an era of Southern history. Admittedly they do not define an end and a beginning so sharply as the events of 1865 or 1877, though we now know that the dramatic suddenness and extent of the changes wrought by those events have been exaggerated. Granting all that, if the earlier eras of revolutionary change can be compared with water-

11

falls in the stream bed of Southern history, then we are perhaps justified in speaking of the most recent era as one of rapids — and fairly precipitous rapids at that.

I / Forgotten Alternatives

IN THE FIRST PLACE it is necessary to clear away some prevailing misconceptions about this latest of lost causes. One of them grows out of a tendency to identify and confuse it with an earlier lost cause. The assumption is often made that Reconstruction constituted an interruption of normal relations between the races in the South. Once the carpetbaggers were overthrown and 'Home Rule' was established, the founding fathers of the New South, after conceding that slavery was finished and the Negro was now a freedman and more vaguely a citizen, are presumed to have restored to normality the disturbed relations between whites and blacks. To conceive of the new order of race relations as a restoration, however, is to forget the nature of relations between races under the old regime. For one thing segregation would have been impractical under slavery, and for another the circumstances that later gave rise to the segregation code did not exist so long as the Negro was enslaved. 'Before and directly after the war,' writes W. E. B. Du Bois, 'when all the best of the Negroes were domestic servants in the best of the white families, there were bonds of intimacy, affection, and sometimes blood relationship, between the races. They lived in the same home, shared in the family life, often attended the same church, and talked and conversed with each other.' These conditions could certainly not be said to have been 're-stored' by segregation.

A second misconception is more common and is shared by a number of historians. While recognizing that the new order was new and not the restoration of an old system, they sometimes make the assumption that it followed automatically upon the overthrow of Reconstruction as an immediate consequence of Redemption. Those who cherish the new order of segregation, Jim Crowism, and disfranchisement, therefore, often attribute it to the Redeemers, the founding fathers of the New South. Their defense of the system clothes it with the moral prestige they attribute to Redemption, and their indignation against any attack upon it is fired by the zeal of the historic struggle for home rule and the emotional heritage of the Civil War period.

14

Their identification of the two causes is understandable but unjustified, and it lingers to complicate and confuse adjustment to the New Reconstruction.

1

AS A MATTER OF FACT, some important aspects of segregation were achieved and sanctioned by the First Reconstruction. One of these was segregation of the great Protestant churches, a process accomplished by the voluntary withdrawal of the Negroes and their establishment of independent organizations of their own. Whatever the intentions of the framers of the Fourteenth Amendment were regarding segregation in the public schools — a controversy that even the Supreme Court in its historic decision of 17 May 1954 declined to settle — the fact is that segregation became the almost universal practice in the public schools of the South during Reconstruction, with or without explicit sanction of the radicals. In a third important field, the military services, segregation was strengthened by the Civil War and left unaltered during Reconstruction. As for equality in social gatherings of a private nature, there is little evidence that even the high Negro officials of Reconstruction governments in the South were extended that recognition — even by the white radicals.

After Redemption was achieved the new governments of the Southern states retained such segregation practices as had been established during or before Reconstruction, but showed little immediate disposition to expand the code into new fields. Much less was there evidence of a movement to make segregation universal, such as it was to become in the twentieth century. More than a decade was to pass after Redemption before the first Jim Crow law was to appear upon the law books of a Southern state, and more than two decades before the older states of Virginia, North Carolina, and South Carolina were to adopt such laws.

Suspicions of the South's intentions toward the freedmen after the withdrawal of federal troops were naturally rife in the North. In 1878 Colonel Thomas Wentworth Higginson went south to investigate for himself. The report of his findings, published in the *Atlantic Monthly,* is of particular interest in view of the Colonel's background. One of the most militant abolitionists, Higginson had been one of the 'Secret Six' who conspired with John Brown before the Harpers Ferry raid, and during the war he had organized and led a combat regiment of Negro troops. In Virginia, South Carolina, and Florida, the states he visited in 1878, he found 'a condition of outward peace' and wondered immediately if there did not lurk beneath it 'some covert plan for crushing or reënslaving the colored race.' If so, he decided, it would 'show itself in some personal ill usage of the blacks, in the withdrawal of privileges, in legislation

16

endangering their rights.' But, he reported, 'I can assert that, carrying with me the eyes of a tolerably suspicious abolitionist, I saw none of these indications.' He had expected to be affronted by contemptuous or abusive treatment of Negroes. 'During this trip,' however, he wrote, 'I had absolutely no occasion for any such attitude.' Nor was this due to 'any cringing demeanor on the part of the blacks, for they show much more manhood than they once did.' He compared the tolerance and acceptance of the Negro in the South on trains and street cars, at the polls, in the courts and legislatures, in the police force and militia, with attitudes in his native New England and decided that the South came off rather better in the comparison. 'How can we ask more of the States formerly in rebellion,' he demanded, 'than that they should be abreast of New England in granting rights and privileges to the colored race? Yet this is now the case in the three states I name; or at least if they fall behind in some points, they lead at some points.' Six years later, in a review of the situation in the South, Higginson found no reason to change his estimate of 1878.

The year 1879 provides testimony to the point from a foreign observer. Sir George Campbell, a member of Parliament, traveled over a large part of the South, with race relations as the focus of his interest. He was impressed with the freedom of association between whites and blacks, with the frequency

17

and intimacy of personal contact, and with the extent of Negro participation in political affairs. He commented with particular surprise on the equality with which Negroes shared public facilities. He remarked that 'the humblest black rides with the proudest white on terms of perfect equality, and without the smallest symptom of malice or dislike on either side. I was, I confess, surprised to see how completely this is the case; even an English Radical is a little taken aback at first.'

In the first year of Redemption a writer who signed himself 'A South Carolinian' in the *Atlantic Monthly* corroborated the observations of the Englishman regarding the Negro's equality of treatment on common carriers, trains, and street cars. 'The negroes are freely admitted to the theatre in Columbia and to other exhibitions, lectures, etc.,' though the whites avoided sitting with them 'if the hall be not crowded,' he added. 'In Columbia they are also served at the bars, soda water fountains, and ice-cream saloons, but not generally elsewhere.'

Twenty years later, in 1897, a Charleston editor referring to a proposed Jim Crow law for trains wrote: 'We care nothing whatever about Northern or outside opinion in this matter. It is a question for our own decision according to our own ideas of what is right and expedient. And our opinion is that we have no more need for a Jim Crow system this year than we had last year, and a great deal less than we had twenty and thirty years ago.' In his view such a law was 'unnecessary and uncalled for,' and furthermore it would be 'a needless affront to our respectable and well behaved colored people.'

Southern white testimony on the subject has naturally been discounted as propaganda. If only by way of contrast with later views, however, the following editorial from the Richmond *Dispatch*, 13 October 1886, is worth quoting: 'Our State Constitution requires all State officers in their oath of office to declare that they "recognize and accept the civil and political equality of all men." We repeat that nobody here objects to sitting in political conventions with negroes. Nobody here objects to serving on juries with negroes. No lawyer objects to practicing law in court where negro lawyers practice . . . Colored men are allowed to introduce bills into the Virginia Legislature; and in both branches of this body negroes are allowed to sit, as they have a right to sit.' George Washington Cable, the aggressive agitator for the rights of Negroes, protested strongly against discrimination elsewhere, but is authority for the statement made in 1885, that 'In Virginia they may ride exactly as white people do and in the same cars.'

More pertinent and persuasive is the testimony of the Negro himself. In April 1885, T. McCants Stewart set forth from Boston to visit his native state of South Carolina after an absence of ten years. A

19

Negro newspaperman, corresponding editor of the New York *Freeman*, Stewart was conscious of his role as a spokesman and radical champion of his race. 'On leaving Washington, D.C.,' he reported to his paper, 'I put a chip on my shoulder, and inwardly dared any man to knock it off.' He found a seat in a car which became so crowded that several white passengers had to sit on their baggage. 'I fairly foamed at the mouth,' he wrote, 'imagining that the conductor would order me into a seat occupied by a colored lady so as to make room for a white passenger.' Nothing of the sort happened, however, nor was there any unpleasantness when Stewart complained of a request from a white Virginian that he shift his baggage so that the white man could sit beside him. At a stop twenty-one miles below Petersburg he entered a station dining room, 'bold as a lion,' he wrote, took a seat at a table with white people, and was courteously served. 'The whites at the table appeared not to note my presence,' he reported. 'Thus far I had found travelling more pleasant . . . than in some parts of New England.' Aboard a steamboat in North Carolina he complained of a colored waiter who seated him at a separate table, though in the same dining room with whites. At Wilmington, however, he suffered from no discrimination in dining arrangements. His treatment in Virginia and North Carolina, he declared, 'contrasted strongly with much that I have experi-

20

enced in dining rooms in the North.' Another contrast that impressed him was the ease and frequency with which white people entered into conversation with him for no other purpose than to pass the time of day. 'I think the whites of the South,' he observed, 'are really less afraid to [have] contact with colored people than the whites of the North.'

Stewart continued his journey southward rejoicing that 'Along the Atlantic seaboard from Canada to the Gulf of Mexico — through Delaware, Maryland, Virginia, the Carolinas, Georgia and into Florida, all the old slave States with enormous Negro populations . . . a first-class ticket is good in a first-class coach; and Mr. [Henry W.] Grady would be compelled to ride with a Negro, or, walk.' From Columbia, South Carolina, he wrote: 'I feel about as safe here as in Providence, R.I. I can ride in first-class cars on the railroads and in the streets. I can go into saloons and get refreshments even as in New York. I can stop in and drink a glass of soda and be more politely waited upon than in some parts of New England.' He also found that 'Negroes dine with whites in a railroad saloon' in his native state. He watched a Negro policeman arrest a white man 'under circumstances requiring coolness, prompt decision, and courage'; and in Charleston he witnessed the review of hundreds of Negro troops. 'Indeed,' wrote Stewart, 'the Palmetto State leads the South in some things. May she go on advancing in liberal

21

practices and prospering throughout her borders, and may she be like leaven to the South; like a star unto "The Land of Flowers," leading our blessed section on and on into the way of liberty, justice, equality, truth, and righteousness.'

One significant aspect of Stewart's newspaper reports should be noted. They were written a month after the inauguration of Grover Cleveland and the return of the Democrats to power for the first time in twenty-four years. His paper had opposed Cleveland, and propaganda had been spread among Negro voters that the return of the Democrats would mean the end of freedmen's rights, if not their liberty. Stewart failed to find what he was looking for, and after a few weeks cut his communications short with the comment that he could find 'nothing spicy or exciting to write.' 'For the life of [me],' he confessed, 'I can't "raise a row" in these letters. Things seem (remember I write seem) to move along as smoothly as in New York or Boston . . . If you should ask me, "watchman, tell us of the night" . . . I would say, "The morning light is breaking." '

So far nearly all the evidence presented has come from the older states of the eastern seaboard. In writing of slavery under the old regime it is common for historians to draw distinctions between the treatment of slaves in the upper and older South and their lot in the lower South and the newer states. In

22

the former their condition is generally said to have been better than it was in the latter. It is worth re-marking an analagous distinction in the treatment of the race in the era of segregation. It is clear at least that the newer states were inclined to resort to Jim Crow laws earlier than the older common-wealths of the seaboard, and there is evidence that segregation and discrimination became generally practiced before they became law. Even so, there are a number of indications that segregation and ostra-cism were not nearly so harsh and rigid in the early years as they became later.

In his study of conditions in Mississippi, Vernon Wharton reveals that for some years 'most of the saloons served whites and Negroes at the same bar. Many of the restaurants, using separate tables, served both races in the same room . . . On May 21, 1879, the Negroes of Jackson, after a parade of their fire company, gave a picnic in Hamilton Park. On the night of May 29, "the ladies of the [white] Episcopal Church" used Hamilton Park for a *fete*. After their picnic the Negroes went to Angelo's Hall for a dance. This same hall was used for white dances and parties, and was frequently the gathering place of Democratic conventions . . . Throughout the state common cemeteries, usually in separate por-tions, held the graves of both whites and Negroes.' Wharton points out, however, that as early as 1890

23

segregation had closed in and the Negroes were by that date excluded from saloons, restaurants, parks, public halls, and white cemeteries.

At the International Exposition in New Orleans in 1885 Charles Dudley Warner watched with some astonishment as 'white and colored people mingled freely, talking and looking at what was of common interest . . . On "Louisiana Day" in the Exposition the colored citizens,' he reported, 'took their full share of the parade and the honors. Their societies marched with the others, and the races mingled in the grounds in unconscious equality of privileges.' While he was in the city he also saw 'a colored clergyman in his surplice seated in the chancel of the most important white Episcopal church in New Orleans, assisting the service.'

A frequent topic of comment by Northern visitors during the period was the intimacy of contact between the races in the South, an intimacy sometimes admitted to be distasteful to the visitor. Standard topics were the sight of white babies suckled at black breasts, white and colored children playing together, the casual proximity of white and Negro homes in the cities, the camaraderie of maidservant and mistress, employer and employee, customer and clerk, and the usual stories of cohabitation of white men and Negro women. The same sights and stories had once been favorite topics of comment for the carpetbaggers and before them of the abolitionists,

24

both of whom also expressed puzzlement and sometimes revulsion. What the Northern traveler of the
'eighties sometimes took for signs of a new era of
race relations was really a heritage of slavery times,
or, more elementally, the result of two peoples having lived together intimately for a long time and
learned to like and trust each other—whatever their
formal relations were, whether those of master and
slave, exploiter and exploited, or superior and inferior.

It would certainly be preposterous to leave the
impression that any evidence I have submitted indicates a golden age of race relations in the period
between Redemption and segregation. On the contrary, the evidence of race conflict and violence, brutality and exploitation in this very period is overwhelming. It was, after all, in the 'eighties and early
'nineties that lynching attained the most staggering
proportions ever reached in the history of that
crime. Moreover, the fanatical advocates of racism,
whose doctrines of total segregation, disfranchisement, and ostracism eventually triumphed over all
opposition and became universal practice in the
South, were already at work and already beginning
to establish dominance over some phases of Southern life. Before their triumph was complete, however, there transpired a period of history whose
significance has been hitherto neglected. Exploitation there was in that period, as in other periods

and in other regions, but it did not follow then that the exploited had to be ostracized. Subordination there was also, unmistakable subordination; but it was not yet an accepted corollary that the subordinates had to be totally segregated and needlessly humiliated by a thousand daily reminders of their subordination. Conflict there was, too, violent conflict in which the advantage lay with the strong and the dominant, as always; but conflict of some kind was unavoidable short of forceful separation of the races.

2

BEFORE THE SOUTH CAPITULATED completely to the doctrines of the extreme racists, three alternative philosophies of race relations were put forward to compete for the region's adherence and support. One of these, the conservative philosophy, attracted wide support and was tried out in practice over a considerable period of time. The second approach to the problem, that of the Southern radicals, received able expression and won numerous adherents, but the lack of political success on the part of the radical party of Populism limited the trial by practice of that philosophy to rather inconclusive experiments. The liberal philosophy of race relations, the third approach, received able and forceful expression, but was promptly and almost totally rejected and never put to practice in that period. All three of these alternative philosophies rejected the

26

doctrines of extreme racism and all three were indigenously and thoroughly Southern in origin.

That was true even of the rejected liberal philosophy of George Washington Cable, almost its sole exponent in this period. For Cable had the right, as he said, to speak 'as a citizen of an extreme Southern State, a native of Louisiana, an ex-Confederate soldier, and a lover of my home, my city, and my State, as well as of my country.' He felt that he belonged 'peculiarly to the South,' he said. 'I had shared in every political error of the "Southerner," and had enjoyed whatever benefits the old slaveholding civilization had to offer. A resultant duty bound me to my best conception of the true interest of the South as a whole — the whole South, white and black.' His book, *The Silent South,* published in 1885, was as eloquent, thoroughgoing, and uncompromising a statement of the liberal position on race as appeared anywhere in the nineteenth century. Cable boldly challenged the Redeemers' philosophy that the South must have 'honest' government before it could aspire to 'free' government, and maintained that there could be neither free nor honest government without equal rights and protection for all citizens — black as well as white. He extended his demand for equality beyond the political sphere and fought discrimination in employment and the administration of justice. He was an outspoken enemy of segregation and the incipient Jim

Crowism of his time. Yet acceptance of his doctrine had to await the development of urban liberalism in the South, which did not arrive in any force until the second quarter of the twentieth century. Our concern here, therefore, is with the other two schools and particularly with that of the conservatives.

The conservative position never received so articulate and explicit an expression as Cable gave the liberal philosophy. The tenets of conservatism have to be derived from fragmentary formulations and from policies pursued. The conservative thought of himself as occupying a position between the doctrinaire Negrophile of the left and the fanatical Negrophobe of the right. On the left were the false friends of the freedman, whose zeal for pushing him ahead of himself, for elevating him beyond his proper station in life, and for placing him in high places he was not prepared to fill had brought about his downfall. They were false friends not only because of an error of judgment but also out of baseness of motive; for they had used their pretended friendship to advance selfish ends of party advantage and private gain. At the opposite pole were the Negrophobe fanatics of the South, who were not satisfied to stop with 'Home Rule' and white government, but would wage aggressive war on the Negro, strip him of basic rights guaranteed him by the Constitution, ostracize him, humiliate him, and rob him of elemental human dignity.

The conservatives reminded the Negro that he had something to lose as well as something to gain and that his Northern champions' exclusive pre-occupation with gains for the Negro had evoked the danger of losing all he had so far gained. The conservative's primary purpose was to conserve. 'The better class of whites,' Wade Hampton told Sir George Campbell, 'certainly want to conserve the negro.' Like other conservatives of the period, the Southern conservatives believed that every properly regulated society had superiors and subordinates, that each class should acknowledge its responsibilities and obligations, and that each should be guaranteed its status and protected in its rights. The conservatives acknowledged that the Negroes belonged in a subordinate role, but denied that subordinates had to be ostracized; they believed that the Negro was inferior, but denied that it followed that inferiors must be segregated or publicly humiliated. Negro degradation was not a necessary corollary of white supremacy in the conservative philosophy.

A blunt and artless statement of the conservative position is found in the words of Governor Thomas G. Jones, leader of the conservative wing of the Democratic party of Alabama in the 'nineties. 'The Negro race is under us,' said the Governor. 'He is in our power. We are his custodians . . . we should extend to him, as far as possible, all the civil rights that will fit him to be a decent and self respecting, law-abiding and intelligent citizen . . . If we do not lift them up, they will drag us down.'

It was clearly an aristocratic philosophy of paternalism and *noblesse oblige* that the conservatives preached, and it was inevitable that the attitude should have acquired class associations in the mind of both its advocates and its opponents. When Hampton told Campbell that 'the better class of whites' sought to conserve the Negroes, he added that 'the lower whites are less favorable.' In 1879 a Columbia, South Carolina, editor (quoted by George B. Tindall) put the case too strongly, perhaps, but registered a common view. 'The old slave owner . . . feels no social fear of negro equality,' he wrote. 'He feels no desire to maltreat and browbeat and spit upon the colored man. He feels no opposition to the education and elevation of the black man in the scale of civilized life.' In the conservative mind distinctions of class sometimes took priority over distinctions of race. Thus in 1885 a Charleston paper remarked that, 'It is a great deal pleasanter to travel with respectable and well-behaved colored people than with unmannerly and ruffianly white men.' And twelve years later the same paper said: 'The common sense and proper arrangement, in our opinion, is to provide first-class cars for first-class passengers, white and colored . . . To speak plainly, we need, as everybody knows, separate cars or apartments for rowdy or drunken white passengers far more than Jim Crow cars for colored passengers.'

An excessive squeamishness or fussiness about contact with Negroes was commonly identified as a lower-class white attitude, while the opposite attitude was as popularly associated with 'the quality.' When some militiamen of Alabama and Mississippi refused in 1887 to attend a national drill in Washington because Negro troops were to participate, a Jacksonville, Florida, paper chided them as having 'dropped a little behind the spirit of the age.' The editor observed that 'when it comes to adopting a standard of conduct in relation to the treatment of the color question . . . it is more likely that the example of the F. F. V.s will prevail over that of these spirited sons of Alabama and Mississippi. We do not expect *Fitzhugh Lee* to make a blunder in this connection.' And when the same year Negroes protested the discriminatory policy adopted by a Florida railroad, an official of the road replied that the policy 'had to be shaped to suit the crackers, as the road ran through a good deal of territory settled by that class.'

Negroes themselves were perfectly well aware of class differences among whites in this matter of race prejudice. It was this difference that the Negro Congressman John R. Lynch of Mississippi had in mind in his speech on the Civil Rights bill in 1875. 'The

31

opposition to civil rights in the South,' he said, 'is not so general or intense as a great many would have the country believe. It is a mistaken idea that all of the white people in the South outside of the republican party are bitterly opposed to this bill.' And he pointed to L. Q. C. Lamar, 'my eloquent and distinguished colleague on the other side of the House' as an example of the 'intelligent legislators and well-bred gentlemen' of the opposition in his state. After listening to a debate in the Virginia Assembly in 1877, J. L. M. Curry recorded in his diary with obvious gratification that 'A negro member said that he and his race relied for the protection of their rights & liberties, not on the "poor white trash" but on the "well-raised" gentlemen.' In 1890, when the demand for Jim Crow legislation was rising, the editor of a Negro periodical in North Carolina wrote: 'The best people of the South do not demand this separate car business'; and again, 'this whole thing is but a pandering to the lower instincts of the worst class of whites in the South.'

When Northern liberals and radicals began to lose interest in the freedmen's cause and federal protection was withdrawn, it was natural that the Negro should turn to the conservatives among upper-class Southerners for allies. While there was a certain amount of fawning Uncle-Tomism among the Negroes, there is little doubt that the prouder of them secretly despised the patronizing pose and self-flattering paternalism of the whites with whom they found refuge. It was no sentimentality for 'Ole Marster' that inspired the freedmen, but the hot breath of cracker fanaticism they felt on the back of their necks.

It would be a mistake to picture the Democratic Redeemers as the first Southern whites to appeal successfully to the Negro voter with the conservative race philosophy. That distinction belongs to the conservative ex-Whig planters of Mississippi, turned Republicans, who took over the party from the radicals and dominated it for several years with Negro support. James L. Alcorn, wealthy planter of the delta, large slaveholder, and quite as much the aristocrat as Wade Hampton or Jefferson Davis, appealed to the Negro with a program of civil rights, legal equality, and public education. The Negro vote plus the ex-Whig support elected Alcorn the first Republican governor of Mississippi, sent him to the Senate for a term, and put another Whig-Republican in the governor's office to succeed Alcorn.

During the electoral crisis of 1876–7 the advisors of Rutherford B. Hayes assured him that 'in almost every Southern State you can find men like Alcorn in Mississippi.' Most of these ex-Whigs of the South had drifted into the Democratic party, after some experiments with the Republicans. The outspoken discontent of the old Whigs with their new party

33

and the acute unhappiness of the Southern Democrats with the policies of the Northern Democrats led Hayes and his advisors to hope that withdrawal of support from the carpetbaggers would leave the old Whigs heirs to the freedmen's votes and encourage them to establish strong conservative Republican movements in the South similar to Alcorn's in Mississippi. High hope for such a political development was one among several reasons that enabled conservative Republicans and Southern Democrats to agree on the Compromise of 1877 that made Hayes President. As it turned out, the Southern ex-Whigs disappointed Hayes, for instead of leading a Republican revolt in the South they went far toward consolidating their control over the Democratic party in that region. To the conservative party, as the Democratic party came to be called in the South, the new leaders brought their Whiggish notions of economics and politics, and along with them their conservative race philosophy.

One tenet of that philosophy was an endorsement and defense of Negro suffrage. In a symposium published in the *North American Review* in 1879, Hampton, Lamar, and Alexander Stephens agreed not only that the disfranchisement of the freedman was impossible, but that even if it were possible the South would not desire it. Hampton had often boasted that he was 'the first white man in the South, after the Civil War, to advocate giving the Negro the franchise' and once declared his belief that 'a large majority of the intelligent and reflecting whites' agreed with him on the subject. In the symposium he declared that 'As the negro becomes more intelligent, he naturally allies himself with the more conservative of the whites.'

The impression often left by cursory histories of the subject is that Negro disfranchisement followed quickly if not immediately upon the overthrow of Reconstruction. It is perfectly true that Negroes were often coerced, defrauded, or intimidated, but they continued to vote in large numbers in most parts of the South for more than two decades after Reconstruction. In the judgment of the abolitionist Higginson, 'The Southern whites accept them precisely as Northern men in cities accept the ignorant Irish vote, — not cheerfully, but with acquiesence in the inevitable; and when the strict color-line is once broken they are just as ready to conciliate the negro as the Northern politician to flatter the Irishman. Any powerful body of voters may be cajoled today and intimidated tomorrow and hated always, but it can never be left out of sight.' As a voter the Negro was both hated and cajoled, both intimidated and courted, but he could never be ignored so long as he voted.

The governors of the last two states redeemed from the carpetbaggers were both on record with unqualified pledges to protect the freedmen in the enjoyment of their rights. The pledges of Governor Hampton of South Carolina and Governor Francis T. Nicholls of Louisiana were made not only to the Republican administration but to the Negro voters of their states. 'After I was recognized as Governor,' wrote Nicholls in his autobiography, 'I set myself earnestly to work to bring about good feeling and confidence between the races . . . I was particularly anxious by kindness and strict justice & impartiality to the colored people . . . that they should feel that they were not proscribed & to this end appointed a number of them to small offices sandwiching them on Boards between white men while they were powerless to do harm they were in a position to see & know everything that was going on.' A white supporter claimed with obvious exaggeration that Nicholls gave the Negroes more recognition and offices in the first year of his administration than the Republicans of Louisiana had given them in their entire regime.

Hampton went further than Nicholls in his efforts to conciliate the freedmen, reconcile the races, and attract Negro voters to the support of his administration. The title of a Hampton campaign book was *Free Men! Free Ballots!! Free Schools!!! The Pledges of Gen. Wade Hampton . . . to the Colored People of South Carolina, 1865–1876.* The computation of a reliable source shows that Hampton appointed at least eighty-six Negroes to office during his administration. None of them was appointed to an important state office, but they were named trial justices, jury commissioners, and members of county and state commissions. Five months after the new government took control, the Republican ex-Governor Robert K. Scott told Northern newspapermen that 'Hampton is honestly carrying out the promises he made during the campaign. He has already appointed more colored men to office than were appointed during the first two years that I was Governor.' Negroes were placed on Democratic tickets as candidates for the legislature in several counties, they were admitted to membership in agricultural societies in a few instances, and their militia companies, fire brigades, and other organizations were encouraged to participate in public functions and demonstrations. The governor's policies won praise from Negro and Republican leaders of South Carolina of that period and have convinced George B. Tindall, a careful historian, that Hampton was 'a generous and constructive statesman with regard to race relations.' His policy proved to be a failure as a political solution, for not even Hampton's great prestige could long keep at bay the Negrophobe element of his own party. After he left the state to go to the Senate the opposition grew until it eventually repudiated his conciliatory policies along with the conservative race philosophy and ended in all-out aggression against the Negro.

37

If the Negro's affinity for the conservative whites had its practical motivations of self interest, so did the conservative interest in the Negro. The tradition of *noblesse oblige* and the flattery of paternalistic impulses do not adequately account for the pains the conservative Redeemers took to conciliate the Negroes and attract their support. The fact was that many of the Whiggish policies of the Redeemers, particularly their subservience to railroads, corporations, and business interests, and their support of financial and monetary doctrines of the Northeast, were highly unpopular in the South — especially among the depressed agricultural white population. Calling themselves Independents, Greenbackers, or Readjusters, these disaffected elements organized in third parties and challenged the control of the conservative Democrats in almost every Southern state shortly after Redemption. They presented a serious threat to conservative control in some states, and in Virginia, where they combined with a wing of the Republican party there, they overthrew the Redeemer government and took over the state. In this situation conservatives were obviously in need of friends, and as the third party grew in other states and threatened to repeat the Virginia tactics, the conservatives naturally sought an understanding with the Negroes.

This understanding or alliance as it worked out in Mississippi under the leadership of Lamar and

Senator J. Z. George was known as the 'fusion principle.' This was a working agreement by which the conservatives helped the Negro wing of the Republican party against the white wing in return for Negro assistance to the conservatives in their struggles against dissident whites — Greenbackers or Republicans, who often worked together. In practice, the county Democratic executive committee would agree with Negro leaders upon the number of offices to be held by Negroes. The proportion and type of offices varied, but usually the Negroes were assigned the less important offices and one of the county's seats in the state legislature. Sometimes they got considerably more, sometimes less. In addition Lamar and the rest of the Democratic congressional delegation used their influence and votes in Washington to secure federal patronage and office for their Negro friends, patronage that would not have gone to Democrats in any case and might have gone to white Republicans. On the motion of Lamar, for example, Blanche K. Bruce, former Negro Senator from Mississippi, was unanimously confirmed as Register of the Treasury. The advantage thus gained by the conservatives consisted in Negro support in local politics against the Independent party, made up of dissident whites of both the old parties. Other advantages lay in keeping the Republicans split, preventing able white leadership from gaining control, and in being able to discredit the Republican party as being under Negro control. Using these tactics, as well as the cruder ones of fraud and terror, the conservatives weathered the Independent and Greenbacker revolts of the early 'eighties. Conservatives of other Southern states who were faced with the same kind of revolt also marshaled the Negro vote against white discontent, using variations of the Mississippi tactics.

Seeing the Independent revolt in the South as an opportunity to split the white vote and restore Republican power in the region, President Chester A. Arthur withdrew his support from the Negro leaders and sought to place native whites in command. Embitterment of Negro voters over this and other Republican policies since 1877 led conservative leaders of the Southern Democrats to attempt a concerted drive to attract them away from their traditional party. The Negro voters were therefore courted, flattered, 'mistered,' and honored by Southern white politicians in the 'eighties as never before. With the cordial recommendation of Southern Democrats, President Cleveland appointed several Negroes to office in the South. Senator E. C. Walthall urged the appointment of one in Mississippi, Senator M. C. Butler in South Carolina, and Senator Isham Harris in Tennessee. Congressman Thomas C. Catchings of Mississippi boasted that by the workings of the 'fusion principle' there were 'more colored men holding office in my district

40

alone, through the action of the Democratic party, than there are in the whole North.'

Caught between the 'Lily-White' policy of the Republican party and the blandishments of the Southern Democrats, the Negro became confused and politically apathetic. Republican organizations declined in strength in the South and many state parties ceased to put forth tickets altogether. Despite that, the Negroes did not flock to the opposing party. For one thing they knew from long experience that, for all their kind words and blandishments, the Democrats would resort to force or fraud in a pinch. For another, Negro leaders were beginning to think in economic terms and ask their people what they had in common with their white landlords, creditors, and employers that would justify a political alliance with the conservatives.

3

THE CONSERVATIVE PHILOSOPHY of race relations was not the only alternative to extreme racism and proscription offered to the South and tried out in practice by Southern white people. Another approach was that of the Southern radicals, as worked out and expressed by the Populists. The agrarian forerunners of the Populists — the Readjusters, Independents, and Greenbackers — also attempted to reach an understanding with the Negro, but they approached him through his Republican leaders to seek a pragmatic alliance of mutual political convenience. They rarely approached him directly and did not seek to convert him personally to their cause. The Populists eventually resorted in large measure to the same tactics. But first they went over the heads of the established leaders, largely Republican, and sought to convert the Negroes themselves, make them good Populists by conviction, fire them with the zeal they themselves felt for the common cause, integrate them thoroughly with the party, and give them a sense of belonging and tangible evidence that they did belong.

The Populists steered clear of the patronizing approach that both the radical Republicans and the conservative Democrats took toward the freedmen. They neither pictured themselves as the keepers of the liberal conscience and the Negro as the ward of the nation, as did the Republican radicals, nor did they assume the pose of *noblesse oblige* and regard the Negro as an object of paternalistic protection as did the Southern conservatives. The Populists fancied themselves as exponents of a new realism on race, free from the delusions of doctrinaire and sentimental liberalism on the one hand, and the illusions of romantic paternalism on the other. There was in the Populist approach to the Negro a limited type of equalitarianism quite different from that preached by the radical Republicans and wholly absent from the conservative approach. This was an equalitarianism of want and poverty, the kinship of a common grievance and a common oppressor. As a Texas Populist expressed the new equalitarianism, 'They are in the ditch just like we are.'

Dismissing irrational motives as of no great account, the Populists grounded their 'realism' on the doctrine that 'self-interest always controls' — the dubious postulate on which much economic and political thought of their day was based. As Tom Watson, foremost leader of Southern Populism, framed the credo: 'Gratitude may fail; so may sympathy, and friendship, and generosity, and patriotism, but, in the long run, self-interest always controls. Let it once appear plainly that it is to the interest of a colored man to vote with the white man and he will do it . . . The People's party will settle the race question. First, by enacting the Australian ballot system. Second, by offering to white and black a rallying point which is free from the odium of former discords and strifes. Third, by presenting a platform immensely beneficial to both races and injurious to neither. Fourth, by making it to the interest of both races to act together for the success of the platform.'

Deprecate emotional and irrational factors of prejudice as they did, the Populist strategists were perfectly aware that these factors were the most serious of all obstacles to their success in the South. It was even more difficult for them than for the conservatives to defy and circumvent race prejudice,

43

since it ran highest and strongest among the very white elements to which the Populist appeal was especially addressed — the depressed lower economic classes. They were the classes from whose phobias and fanaticisms the conservatives offered to protect the Negro. To master these deep-rooted phobias and create a community of feeling and interest in which the two races could combine required greater political genius than the conservatives had to muster for their program. The wonder is not that the Populists eventually failed but that they made as much headway as they did against the overwhelming odds they faced.

The measures they took were sometimes drastic and, for the times, even heroic. At a time when Georgia led all the states in lynchings Watson announced that it was the object of his party to 'make lynch law odious to the people.' And in 1896 the Populist platform of Georgia contained a plank denouncing lynch law. In the campaign of 1892 a Negro Populist who had made sixty-three speeches for Watson was threatened with lynching and fled to him for protection. Two thousand armed white farmers, some of whom rode all night, responded to Watson's call for aid and remained on guard for two nights at his home to avert the threat of violence.

Addressing himself directly to the problem of color prejudice, Watson told the two races: 'You are made to hate each other because upon that hatred is rested the keystone of the arch of financial despotism which enslaves you both. You are deceived and blinded that you may not see how this race antagonism perpetuates a monetary system which beggars you both.' Repeatedly he stressed the identity of interests that transcended differences in race, telling them that 'the colored tenant . . . is in the same boat with the white tenant, the colored laborer with the white laborer,' and that 'the accident of color can make no difference in the interests of farmers, croppers, and laborers.' He promised the Negroes that 'if you stand up for your rights and for your manhood, if you stand shoulder to shoulder with us in this fight' the People's party will 'wipe out the color line and put every man on his citizenship irrespective of color.'

To implement their promises the radicals went further in the direction of racial integration than did the conservatives. 'We have no disposition to ostracize the colored people,' declared the president of the first Populist convention in Texas. 'I am in favor of giving the colored man full representation . . . He is a citizen just as much as we are, and the party that acts on that fact will gain the colored vote of the south.' The convention cheered these sentiments and elected two Negroes to the state executive committee of the party. Other Southern states followed the example of Texas. Negroes were not put off with nominal duties and peripheral appointments, but were taken into the inmost councils of the party. They served with Southern whites as members of state, district, and county executive committees, campaign committees, and delegations to national conventions. Black and white campaigners spoke from the same platform to audiences of both races, and both had their places on official party tickets. Populist sheriffs saw to it that Negroes appeared for jury duty; and Populist editors sought out achievements of Negroes to praise in their columns.

In the opinion of Henry Demarest Lloyd, the Southern Populists gave 'negroes of the South a political fellowship which they have never obtained, not even from their saviors, the Republicans.' Certain it is that the Negroes responded with more enthusiasm and hope than to any other political movement since their disillusionment with radical Republicanism. It is altogether probable that during the brief Populist upheaval of the 'nineties Negroes and native whites achieved a greater comity of mind and harmony of political purpose than ever before or since in the South.

The obvious danger in this account of the race policies of Southern conservatives and radicals is one of giving an exaggerated impression of interracial harmony. There were Negrophobes among the radicals as well as among the conservatives, and there were hypocrites and dissemblers in both camps. The politician who flatters to attract votes is a familiar figure in all parties, and the discrepancy between platforms and performance is often as wide as the gap between theory and practice, or the contrast between ethical ideals and everyday conduct.

My only purpose has been to indicate that things have not always been the same in the South. In a time when the Negroes formed a much larger proportion of the population than they did later, when slavery was a live memory in the minds of both races, and when the memory of the hardships and bitterness of Reconstruction was still fresh, the race policies accepted and pursued in the South were sometimes milder than they became later. The policies of proscription, segregation, and disfranchisement that are often described as the immutable 'folkways' of the South, impervious alike to legislative reform and armed intervention, are of a more recent origin. The effort to justify them as a consequence of Reconstruction and a necessity of the times is embarrassed by the fact that they did not originate in those times. And the belief that they are immutable and unchangeable is not supported by history.

II / Capitulation to Racism

UP TO THE YEAR 1898 South Carolina had resisted the Jim Crow car movement which had swept the western states of the South completely by that time. In that year, however, after several attempts, the proponents of the Jim Crow law were on the eve of victory. The Charleston *News and Courier*, the oldest newspaper in the South and a consistent spokesman of conservatism, fired a final broadside against extremists in behalf of the conservative creed of race policy.

'As we have got on fairly well for a third of a century, including a long period of reconstruction, without such a measure,' wrote the editor, 'we can probably get on as well hereafter without it, and certainly so extreme a measure should not be

49

adopted and enforced without added and urgent cause.' He then called attention to what he considered the absurd consequences to which such a law might lead once the principle of the thing were conceded. 'If there must be Jim Crow cars on the railroads, there should be Jim Crow cars on the street railways. Also on all passenger boats. . . . If there are to be Jim Crow cars, moreover, there should be Jim Crow waiting saloons at all stations, and Jim Crow eating houses. . . . There should be Jim Crow sections of the jury box, and a separate Jim Crow dock and witness stand in every court — and a Jim Crow Bible for colored witnesses to kiss. It would be advisable also to have a Jim Crow section in county auditors' and treasurers' offices for the accommodation of colored taxpayers. The two races are dreadfully mixed in these offices for weeks every year, especially about Christmas. . . . There should be a Jim Crow department for making returns and paying for the privileges and blessings of citizenship. Perhaps, the best plan would be, after all, to take the short cut to the general end . . . by establishing two or three Jim Crow counties at once, and turning them over to our colored citizens for their special and exclusive accommodation.'

In resorting to the tactics of *reductio ad absurdum* the editor doubtless believed that he had dealt the Jim Crow principle a telling blow with his heavy irony. But there is now apparent to us an irony in his argument of which the author was unconscious. For what he intended as a *reductio ad absurdum* and obviously regarded as an absurdity became in a very short time a reality, and not only that but a reality that was regarded as the only sensible solution to a vexing problem, a solution having the sanction of tradition and long usage. Apart from the Jim Crow counties and the Jim Crow witness stand, all the improbable applications of the principle suggested by the editor in derision had been put into practice — down to and including the Jim Crow Bible.

The South's adoption of extreme racism was due not so much to a conversion as it was to a relaxation of the opposition. All the elements of fear, jealousy, proscription, hatred, and fanaticism had long been present, as they are present in various degrees of intensity in any society. What enabled them to rise to dominance was not so much cleverness or ingenuity as it was a general weakening and discrediting of the numerous forces that had hitherto kept them in check. The restraining forces included not only Northern liberal opinion in the press, the courts, and the government, but also internal checks imposed by the prestige and influence of the Southern conservatives, as well as by the idealism and zeal of the Southern radicals. What happened toward the end of the century was an almost simultaneous — and sometimes not unrelated — decline in the effectiveness of restraint that had been exercised by all three forces: Northern liberalism, Southern conservatism, and Southern radicalism.

1

THE ACQUIESCENCE of Northern liberalism in the Compromise of 1877 defined the beginning, but not the ultimate extent, of the liberal retreat on the race issue. The Compromise merely left the freedman to the custody of the conservative Redeemers upon their pledge that they would protect him in his constitutional rights. But as these pledges were forgotten or violated and the South veered toward proscription and extremism, Northern opinion shifted to the right, keeping pace with the South, conceding point after point, so that at no time were the sections very far apart on race policy. The failure of the liberals to resist this trend was due in part to political factors. Since reactionary politicians and their cause were identified with the bloody-shirt issue and the demagogic exploitation of sectional animosities, the liberals naturally felt themselves strongly drawn toward the cause of sectional reconciliation. And since the Negro was the symbol of sectional strife, the liberals joined in deprecating further agitation of his cause and in defending the Southern view of race in its less extreme forms. It was quite common in the 'eighties and 'nineties to find in the *Nation, Harper's Weekly,* the *North American Review,* or the *Atlantic Monthly* Northern liberals and former abolitionists mouthing the shibboleths of white supremacy regarding the Negro's innate inferiority, shiftlessness, and hopeless unfitness for full participation in the white man's civilization. Such expressions doubtless did much to add to the reconciliation of North and South, but they did so at the expense of the Negro. Just as the Negro gained his emancipation and new rights through a falling out between white men, he now stood to lose his rights through the reconciliation of white men.

The cumulative weakening of resistance to racism was expressed also in a succession of decisions by the United States Supreme Court between 1873 and 1898 that require no review here. In the *Slaughter House Cases* of 1873 and in *United States* v. *Reese* and *United States* v. *Cruikshank* in 1876, the court drastically curtailed the privileges and immunities recognized as being under federal protection. It continued the trend in its decision on the *Civil Rights Cases* of 1883 by virtually nullifying the restrictive parts of the Civil Rights Act. By a species of what Justice Harlan in his dissent described as 'subtle and ingenious verbal criticism,' the court held that the Fourteenth Amendment gave Congress power to restrain states but not individuals from acts of racial discrimination and segregation. The court, like the liberals, was engaged in a bit of reconciliation — reconciliation between federal and state jurisdiction, as well as between North and South, reconciliation also achieved at the Negro's expense. Having ruled in a previous case (*Hall* v. *de Cuir*, 1877) that a state could not *prohibit* segregation on a common carrier, the Court in 1890 (*Louisville, New Orleans, and Texas Railroad* v. *Mississippi*) ruled that a state could constitutionally *require* segregation on carriers. In *Plessy* v. *Ferguson*, decided in 1896, the Court subscribed to the doctrine that 'legislation is powerless to eradicate racial instincts' and laid down the 'separate but equal' rule for the justification of segregation. Two years later, in 1898, in *Williams* v. *Mississippi* the Court completed the opening of the legal road to proscription, segregation, and disfranchisement by approving the Mississippi plan for depriving Negroes of the franchise.

Then, in that same year, 1898, the United States plunged into imperialistic adventures under the leadership of the Republican party. These adventures in the Pacific and the Caribbean suddenly brought under the jurisdiction of the United States some eight million people of the colored races, 'a varied assortment of inferior races,' as the *Nation* described them, 'which, of course, could not be allowed to vote.' As America shouldered the White Man's Burden she took up at the same time many Southern attitudes on the subject of race. 'If the stronger and cleverer race,' said the editor of the *Atlantic Monthly*, 'is free to impose its will upon "new-caught, sullen peoples" on the other side of the globe, why not in South Carolina and Mississippi?' The doctrines of Anglo-Saxon superiority by which Professor John W. Burgess of Columbia University, Captain Alfred T. Mahan of the United States Navy, and Senator Albert Beveridge of Indiana justified and rationalized American imperialism in the Philippines, Hawaii, and Cuba differed in no essentials from the race theories by which Senator Benjamin R. Tillman of South Carolina and Senator James K. Vardaman of Mississippi justified white supremacy in the South. The Boston Evening *Transcript* of 14 January 1899, admitted that Southern race policy was 'now the policy of the Administration of the very party which carried the country into and through a civil war to free the slave.' And *The New York Times* of 10 May 1900 reported editorially that 'Northern men . . . no longer denounce the suppression of the Negro vote [in the South] as it used to be denounced in the reconstruction days. The necessity of it under the supreme law of self-preservation is candidly recognized.'

In the South leaders of the white-supremacy movement thoroughly grasped and expounded the implication of the new imperialism for their domestic policies. 'No Republican leader,' declared Senator Tillman, 'not even Governor Roosevelt, will now dare to wave the bloody shirt and preach

55

a crusade against the South's treatment of the negro. The North has a bloody shirt of its own. Many thousands of them have been made into shrouds for murdered Filipinos, done to death because they were fighting for liberty.' And the junior Senator from South Carolina, John J. McLaurin, thanked Senator George F. Hoar of Massachusetts 'for his complete announcement of the divine right of the Caucasian to govern the inferior races,' a position which 'most amply vindicated the South.' Hilary A. Herbert, an advocate of complete disfranchisement of the Negro in Alabama rejoiced in May 1900 that 'we have now the sympathy of thoughtful men in the North to an extent that never before existed.'

At the dawn of the new century the wave of Southern racism came in as a swell upon a mounting tide of national sentiment and was very much a part of that sentiment. Had the tide been running the other way, the Southern wave would have broken feebly instead of becoming a wave of the future.

2

WHILE NORTHERN AND NATIONAL RESTRAINTS upon race extremists were relaxing, internal Southern resistance was also crumbling. Such restraining influence as the conservative tradition exercised upon race policy depended in large measure upon the power of Southern conservatives to retain the role of leadership that they had consolidated upon Redemption. They enjoyed enormous prestige for the overthrow of the carpetbaggers, a prestige that tided them over many of their difficulties. They contrived also to surround their regime with the protective mystique of the Lost Cause and to marshal for their support the powerful emotions of sectional patriotism that welled up out of the historic experiences of defeat, military occupation, and common suffering. Exploiting these advantages skillfully, the conservatives prolonged a remarkable tenure of office.

An accumulation of grievances and discontents gradually weakened their claim upon popular loyalty and undermined the authority of the conservative tradition. In the 'eighties a series of financial scandals in the Redeemer governments were exposed and the treasurers of seven states absconded or were charged with misappropriating funds. In some states, particularly Mississippi, the defalcations and pilfering outstripped the record of the carpetbaggers in this respect. Since the propaganda by which the Redeemers justified their overthrow of the carpetbaggers laid great stress upon corruption and dishonesty in office, and since one of the strongest claims of the Redeemers was impeccable honesty, the treasury scandals were especially embarrassing.

Another embarrassment that diminished the contrast between Redemption and Reconstruction was the conservative alliance with the Negro. In order to gain power to overthrow the carpetbaggers, the conservatives had enlisted the support of the aggressively anti-Negro whites in the struggle for redemption. That accomplished, the conservatives then attempted to moderate the passions of their Negrophobe allies and conciliate the freedmen with paternalistic offers of patronage and protection. The 'Straightout' or white-supremacy element often found the conservative tactics of pampering the Negro extremely difficult to stomach. When the General Assembly of North Carolina, under conservative control, elected several Negro magistrates for certain counties, nine white Democratic members signed a vigorous protest against the action as 'inconsistent with the principles and purposes of the party.' One of those principles, repeatedly expressed in the campaign for redemption, had been that Negroes were 'absolutely unfit for these public positions.' And, added the protest, 'If Democrats do what they have persistently abused and condemned Republicans for doing, how can they hope to escape just censure?' The 'Straightout' element of South Carolina, Mississippi, Louisiana, and other states similarly expressed their chagrin and even outrage over the soft race policy pursued by Hampton, Lamar, Nicholls, and their conservative colleagues.

Greater by far than either the financial scandals or the racial politics of the conservatives as a cause of their declining popularity were their economic policies and alliances. The Whiggish doctrines and ante-bellum associations of the Redeemers had never been among their more popular assets, and in the eyes of most Southerners they were liabilities. The Whigs had normally been the minority party aligned against the ante-bellum Democrats. Hamiltonian in outlook, they continued the Federalist tradition, constituted themselves champions of property rights and spokesmen of financial, commercial, and industrial interests. They broadened their appeal somewhat among the humble folk by demagogic devices and their opposition to the secession movement, but they continued to be known as the party of privilege. Before the war they had lent an agrarian ballast to the national party of the businessman. Their influence in the conservative Democratic party after the war, however, had been swung markedly on the side of corporate, industrial, and railroad interests. They struggled successfully to prevent the Southern Democrats from returning to their old alliance with the West and adopting Western notions about money, banks, railroads, and agrarian reforms. They were determined instead to keep the South in step with the conservative Northeastern wing of the party and with its views upon economic policy. Their reasoning was that the South's desperate need for capital and for industrialization justified any means to attract the confidence and interest of investors.

The storm of discontent aroused by the agrarian depression of the 'eighties and 'nineties caught the conservatives off guard and threw them on the defensive. A great restiveness seized upon the populace, a more profound upheaval of economic discontent than had ever moved the Southern people before, more profound in its political manifestations than that which shook them in the Great Depression of the 1930's. 'I call that particular change a revolution,' wrote the Alabama historian William Garrott Brown, who lived through it, 'and I would use a stronger term if there were one; for no other political movement — not that of 1776, nor that of 1860–1861 — ever altered Southern life so profoundly.'

After trying rigid resistance, and appealing to party loyalty, Southern patriotism, and white solidarity without the desired effect, the conservatives bent to the storm to the extent of giving verbal assent to the program of reforms demanded by the aggressive Farmer's Alliance. But when they failed to carry through with their promises and live up to their pledges, the farmers accused them of betraying the cause, hastily organized a third party, and went into all out revolt against the conservatives as well as the party they dominated. The Populists defied not only the conservative leaders but pretty much all they stood for, including the one-party system, the Eastern alliance, and white solidarity.

In their frantic efforts to stop the revolt and save themselves the conservatives lost their heads and sought to re-enact the triumph of earlier years by which they overthrew the carpetbaggers, redeemed the South, and won their laurels. They persuaded themselves that the crisis of the 'nineties was as desperate as that of the 'seventies had been. The South must be redeemed again, and the political ethics of redemption — which justified any means used to achieve the end — were pressed into service against the Populists as they had been against the carpetbaggers. The same means of fraud, intimidation, bribery, violence, and terror were used against the one that had been used against the other. 'I told them to go to it, boys, count them out,' admitted the conservative Governor William C. Oates of Alabama. 'We had to do it. Unfortunately, I say it was a necessity. We could not help ourselves.'

Alarmed by the success that the Populists were enjoying with their appeal to the Negro voter, the conservatives themselves raised the cry of 'Negro domination' and white supremacy, and enlisted the Negrophobe elements. The conservatives had allied themselves with these elements before in the Redemption crisis, and then later, after the crisis was over, they had been able to tame the extremists into moderation. But they could no longer claim in justification that they were using these tactics against an alien element or even against a despised race.

61

They were using them against their own people, Southern white people. 'It is no excuse,' declared a Virginia Populist paper in 1893, 'to say that these iniquities are practiced to "preserve white civilization." In the first place it was white men who were robbed of their votes, and white men who were defrauded out of office.'

The conservatives compounded their offense and further weakened their moral authority with lower-class white men by using the Negro vote against them. For while they were raising a storm of race feeling against the Populists with the charge that the insurgents were using the Negro against the white man's party, the conservatives were taking advantage of their dominance in the Black Belt to pile up huge majorities of Negro votes for the cause of white supremacy. Some of these voters were bought and some intimidated, but in the main they were merely counted for the ticket, however they voted or whether they voted or not. Time after time the Populists would discover that after they had carried the white counties, fraudulent returns from the Black Belt counties padded with ballots the Negro did or did not cast were used to overwhelm them. When the conservatives in 1896 proved able to carry only one-fifth of the parishes of Louisiana that had a white majority, the New Orleans *Times-Democrat* cynically remarked that white supremacy had again been 'saved by negro votes.' The tactics by which the conservatives crushed the Populist revolt completely undermined their moral position on race policy, for their methods had made a mockery of the plea for moderation and fair play.

The Populist experiment in interracial harmony, precarious at best and handicapped from the start by suspicion and prejudice, was another casualty of the political crisis of the 'nineties. While the movement was at the peak of zeal the two races had surprised each other and astonished their opponents by the harmony they achieved and the good will with which they co-operated. When it became apparent that their opponents would stop at nothing to divide them, however, and would steal the Negro's votes anyway, the bi-racial partnership of Populism began to dissolve in frustration and bitterness. Many of the Negroes became apathetic and ceased political activity altogether. Some of the white Populists understood that the Negro was merely one of the hapless victims rather than the author of the party's downfall. But for the majority it came much easier to blame the Negro for their defeat, to make him the scapegoat, and to vent upon him the pent up accumulation of bitterness against the legitimate offenders who had escaped their wrath.

If the psychologists are correct in their hypothesis that aggression is always the result of frustration, then the South toward the end of the 'nineties was the perfect cultural seedbed for aggression against the minority race. Economic, political, and social frustrations had pyramided to a climax of social tensions. No real relief was in sight from the long cyclical depression of the 'nineties, an acute period of suffering that had only intensified the distress of the much longer agricultural depression. Hopes for reform and the political means employed in defiance of tradition and at great cost to emotional attachments to effect reform had likewise met with cruel disappointments and frustration. There had to be a scapegoat. And all along the line signals were going up to indicate that the Negro was an approved object of aggression. These 'permissions-to-hate' came from sources that had formerly denied such permission. They came from the federal courts in numerous opinions, from Northern liberals eager to conciliate the South, from Southern conservatives who had abandoned their race policy of moderation in their struggle against the Populists, from the Populists in their mood of disillusionment with their former Negro allies, and from a national temper suddenly expressed by imperialistic adventures and aggressions against colored peoples in distant lands.

The resistance of the Negro himself had long ceased to be an important deterrent to white aggression. But a new and popular spokesman of the race, its acknowledged leader by the late 'nineties, came forward with a submissive philosophy for the Negro that to some whites must have appeared an invitation to further aggression. It is quite certain that Booker T. Washington did not intend his so-called 'Atlanta Compromise' address of 1895 to constitute such an invitation. But in proposing the virtual retirement of the mass of Negroes from the political life of the South and in stressing the humble and menial role that the race was to play, he would seem unwittingly to have smoothed the path to proscription.

3

HAVING SERVED as the national scapegoat in the reconciliation and reunion of North and South, the Negro was now pressed into service as a sectional scapegoat in the reconciliation of estranged white classes and the reunion of the Solid South. The bitter violence and blood-letting recrimination of the campaigns between white conservatives and white radicals in the 'nineties had opened wounds that could not be healed by ordinary political nostrums and free-silver slogans. The only formula powerful enough to accomplish that was the magical formula of white supremacy, applied without stint and without any of the old conservative reservations of paternalism, without deference to any lingering resistance of Northern liberalism, or any fear of further check from a defunct Southern Populism.

The first step in applying the formula was the total disfranchisement of the Negro. In part this was presented as a guarantee that in the future neither of the white factions would violate the white man's peace by rallying the Negro's support against the other. In part disfranchisement was also presented as a progressive reform, the sure means of purging Southern elections of the corruption that disgraced them. The disgrace and public shame of this corruption were more widely and keenly appreciated than the circuitous and paradoxical nature of the proposed reform. To one Virginian, however, it did seem that disfranchising the Negroes 'to prevent the Democratic election officials from stealing their votes' would be 'to punish the man who has been injured' — a topsy-turvy justice at best. In no mood for paradoxes, Southerners generally accepted Negro disfranchisement as a reform, without taking second thought.

The standard devices for accomplishing disfranchisement on a racial basis and evading the restrictions of the Constitution were invented by Mississippi, a pioneer of the movement and the only state that resorted to it before the Populist revolt took the form of political rebellion. Other states elaborated the original scheme and added devices of their own contriving, though there was a great deal of borrowing and interchange of ideas throughout the South. First of all, the plan set up certain barriers such as property or literacy qualifications for voting, and then cut certain loopholes in the barrier through which only white men could squeeze. The loopholes to appease (though not invariably accommodate) the underprivileged whites were the 'understanding clause,' the 'grandfather clause,' or the 'good character clause.' Some variation of the scheme was incorporated into the constitutions of South Carolina in 1895, Louisiana in 1898, North Carolina in 1900, Alabama in 1901, Virginia in 1902, Georgia in 1908, and Oklahoma in 1910. The restrictions imposed by these devices were enormously effective in decimating the Negro vote, but in addition all these states as well as the remaining members of the old Confederacy — Florida, Tennessee, Arkansas, and Texas — adopted the poll tax. With its cumulative features and procedures artfully devised to discourage payment, the poll tax was esteemed at first by some of its proponents as the most reliable means of curtailing the franchise — not only among the Negroes but among objectionable whites as well.

But if the Negroes did learn to read, or acquire sufficient property, and remember to pay the poll tax and to keep the receipt on file, they could even then be tripped by the final hurdle devised for them — the white primary. Another of the fateful paradoxes that seemed to dog the history of the progressive movement in the South, the primary system was

undoubtedly an improvement over the old convention system and did much to democratize nomina-
tions and party control. But along with the progres-
sively inspired primary system were adopted the
oppositely inspired party rules, local regulations,
and in some cases state laws excluding the minority
race from participation and converting the primary
into a white man's club. This perverse 'reform'
usually followed hard upon, though sometimes
preceded, the disfranchisement 'reform.' The state-
wide Democratic primary was adopted in South
Carolina in 1896, Arkansas in 1897, Georgia in 1898,
Florida and Tennessee in 1901, Alabama and Mississippi in 1902, Kentucky and Texas in 1903, Louisiana in 1906, Oklahoma in 1907, Virginia in 1913,
and North Carolina in 1915.

The effectiveness of disfranchisement is suggested
by a comparison of the number of registered Negro
voters in Louisiana in 1896, when there were
130,334, and in 1904, when there were 1,342. Between the two dates the literacy, property, and poll-
tax qualifications were adopted. In 1896 Negro
registrants were in a majority in twenty-six parishes
— by 1900 in none.

In spite of the ultimate success of disfranchisement, the movement met with stout resistance and
succeeded in some states by narrow margins or the
use of fraud. In order to overcome the opposition
and divert the suspicions of the poor and illiterate

whites that they as well as the Negro were in danger of losing the franchise — a suspicion that often proved justified — the leaders of the movement resorted to an intensive propaganda of white supremacy, Negrophobia, and race chauvinism. Such a campaign preceded and accompanied disfranchisement in each state. In some of them it had been thirty years or more since the reign of the carpetbagger, but the legend of Reconstruction was revived, refurbished, and relived by the propagandists as if it were an immediate background of the current crisis. A new generation of Southerners was as forcibly impressed with the sectional trauma as if they had lived through it themselves. Symbols and paraphernalia of the Redemption drama were patched up and donned by twentieth-century wearers. Boys who had been born since General U. S. Grant was laid in his tomb paraded in the red shirts of their fathers, and popular Southern novelists glamorized the history of the Ku Klux Klan, the Knights of the White Camelia, and the heroes of the struggle for Home Rule.

In Georgia and elsewhere the propaganda was furthered by a sensational press that played up and headlined current stories of Negro crime, charges of rape and attempted rape, and alleged instances of arrogance, impertinence, surly manners, or lack of prompt and proper servility in conduct. Already cowed and intimidated, the race was falsely pictured

69

as stirred up to a mutinous and insurrectionary pitch. The Atlanta *Journal,* edited by Hoke Smith while he was a candidate for governor on a disfranchisement platform, was one of the worst offenders in this regard. Throughout his campaign Smith's paper kept up a daily barrage of Negro atrocity stories.

It was inevitable that race relations should deteriorate rapidly under such pressure. The immediate consequences in two states were bloody mob wars upon the Negro. Shortly after the red-shirt, white-supremacy election of 1898 in North Carolina a mob of four hundred white men led by a former congressman invaded the colored district of Wilmington, set fire to buildings, killed and wounded many Negroes, and chased hundreds out of town. The sequel to Hoke Smith's white-supremacy victory in Georgia in 1906 was a four-day rule of anarchy in Atlanta, during which mobs roved the city freely looting, murdering, and lynching.

This ugly temper did not pass with the white-supremacy campaigns. Indeed the more defenseless, disfranchised, and intimidated the Negro became the more prone he was to the ruthless aggression of mobs. Three years after Tillman had completed his work of crushing Negro rights in South Carolina, colored people were victims of a series of atrocities. While the state had accustomed itself peacefully to dozens of Negro postmasters before, the appoint-

ment of one in 1898 at Lake City touched off a mob
that burned the postmaster up in his own house and
shot down his family as they escaped. The same year
mobs of 'white cap' riders ranged over the country-
side of Greenwood County shooting and hanging
an undetermined number of Negroes. Two years
after the white-supremacy campaign had disfranchised the race in Louisiana, uncontrolled mobs
took over the city of New Orleans and robbed and
assaulted Negroes for three days. The number of
lynchings per year was fortunately on the decline
during the first decade of the century in the country
as a whole and in the South. But the proportion of
lynchings committed in the South was at the same
time increasing, and so was the proportion of Negro
victims of the lynchings committed.

A few of the old conservatives still spoke out
against the savage turn that events had taken in race
relations. Wade Hampton announced during the
disfranchisement campaign in South Carolina that
he had 'no fear of Negro domination,' that the Negroes had 'acted of late with rare moderation,' and
that race prejudice was being exploited for the purposes of demagogues. But Hampton's influence had
waned and he could do nothing to stop the Tillman-
ites. Ex-Governor Oates of Alabama, known as 'a
conservative among conservatives' and once the
nemesis of Populism in his state, declared that he
was shocked at 'the change in public opinion in re-

71

gard to the status of the Negro' that had occurred by 1901. 'Why, sir,' he declared to the disfranchising constitutional convention of Alabama, 'the sentiment is altogether different now, when the Negro is doing no harm, why the people want to kill him and wipe him from the face of the earth.' But it was Governor Oates who had admitted to the same body that in the heat of the Populist revolt he had said, 'Go to it, boys. Count them out.' The admission weakened his moral position, as the conservative tactic generally had undermined the authority of conservative influence on race relations.

Other representatives of the old conservative school, such as Senator John T. Morgan of Alabama, gave aid and comfort to the racists; or like Hoke Smith went over to them lock, stock, and barrel, and became one of their leaders. Younger men whose background, associations, and ideas would have normally drawn them to the conservative, Hamptonian position on race in earlier days — men such as John Sharp Williams of Mississippi, or Furnifold M. Simmons of North Carolina, or later James F. Byrnes of South Carolina — were swept up in the tide of racist sentiment and gave voice to it.

White-supremacy leaders, however, measured their success not by the number of conservative converts to their cause, but by the response of the old Populists. For if the racist strategy for the reconciliation of alienated white men and the restoration of the Solid South were to work, it would have to win the insurgents. Populists were shrewdly watched for their reaction. In 1898, while the Populists were still in control of the North Carolina government, Josephus Daniels reported with elation seeing 'quite a number of white Populists and white Republicans' taking part in a red-shirt parade for white supremacy. The following year when several Populist members of the Legislature cast their votes for the disfranchisement amendment, 'the applause was long and deafening, shouts and yells being added to the hand clapping.' The reported yells were probably of the well-known 'rebel' variety, for they hailed a closing of the white man's ranks — white solidarity again.

Tom Watson, Populist candidate for President in 1904, was slower than some of his party to close ranks on the race issue and capitulate to the extremists. He had indignantly denounced the South Carolina disfranchisement campaign in 1895 with the statement that 'All this reactionary legislation is wrong' and that 'Old fashioned democracy taught that a man who fought the battles of his country, and paid the taxes of his government, should have a vote.' Bruised and embittered by another decade of futile battles, he still believed that 'the bugaboo of negro domination' was 'the most hypocritical that unscrupulous leadership could invent.' But by 1906 he had persuaded himself that only after the Negro was eliminated from politics could Populist principles gain a hearing. In other words, the white men would have to unite before they could divide. Watson optimistically believed that disfranchisement was the way to break up, rather than to unite, the Solid South. With that in view he offered to swing the Populist vote to any progressive Democratic candidate for governor who would run pledged to a platform of Populist reforms and Negro disfranchisement. Hoke Smith, a recent convert to progressivism from conservative ranks, took up the challenge and Watson delivered the Populist vote, with the results we have already reviewed. The picture of the Georgia Populist and the reformed Georgia conservative united on a platform of Negrophobia and progressivism was strikingly symbolical of the new era in the South. The campaign made Watson the boss of Georgia politics, but it wrote off Populism as a noble experiment, and launched its leader as one of the outstanding exploiters of endemic Negrophobia.

The omission of the South from the annals of the progressive movement has been one of the glaring oversights of American historians. Not only were all phases and aspects of the movement acted out below the Mason and Dixon line, but in some particulars the Southern progressives anticipated and exceeded the performance of their counterparts in the West and East. They chalked up some spectacular gains

74

against the bosses and machines, the corporations and railroads, the insurance companies and trusts. They democratized politics with direct and preferential primaries, with corrupt-practices and anti-lobby acts, with initiative and referendum. They scored gains in humanitarian legislation for miners, factory workers, child labor, and the consumer.

The blind spot in the Southern progressive record — as, for that matter, in the national movement — was the Negro, for the whole movement in the South coincided paradoxically with the crest of the wave of racism. Still more important to the association of the two movements was the fact that their leaders were often identical. In fact, the typical progressive reformer rode to power in the South on a disfranchising or white-supremacy movement. Hoke Smith of Georgia is a case in point, but there were others. Charles B. Aycock and Josephus Daniels of North Carolina are two instances, and Carter Glass and Andrew J. Montague of Virginia are two more. And even those Southern progressives who gained power after the white-supremacy movement had triumphed — as was the case with Napoleon B. Broward of Florida and Braxton B. Comer of Alabama — were indebted to the movement, built upon it, and never repudiated it.

Racism was conceived of by some as the very foundation of Southern progressivism. Edgar Gardner Murphy, one of the most articulate and cultured of Southern progressives, thought of 'the conscious unity of race' as 'the broader ground of the new democracy,' and believed that despite all its limitations it was 'better as a basis of democratic reorganization than the distinctions of wealth, of trade, of property, of family, or class.' He praised 'the deep sociological value of what has been called "race prejudice" ' even though he earnestly deplored some of its results. Thomas P. Bailey, a Southern educator, conceived of progressivism as a direct corollary of racial proscription in the South. *'In fine,'* he wrote, *'disfranchisement of the negroes has been concomitant with the growth of political and social solidarity among the whites.* The more white men recognize sharply their kinship with their fellow whites, and the more democracy in every sense of the term spreads among them, the more the negro is compelled to "keep his place" — a place that is gradually narrowing in the North as well as in the South.'

The success of Woodrow Wilson's campaign for the presidential nomination and the management and direction of his race for President were in very considerable degree the work of an able school of Southern progressive politicians. Likewise the striking success of the progressive reforms of Wilson's first administration owed much of their vigor to the work of Southern cabinet members and congressional leaders. These Southern progressives also brought along to Washington with them the racial doctrines that left their stamp on the Wilsonian progressivism. One month before the election of Wilson, Josephus Daniels, then in charge of the publicity bureau of the Presidential campaign and soon to become a member of Wilson's cabinet, published an editorial in his North Carolina paper in which he said that the South would never feel secure until the North and West had adopted the whole Southern policy of political proscription and social segregation of the Negro.

4

PARTISAN POLITICS was not the only index of the new trend in Southern race policy. A look at the contrast between Southern letters in the 1880's and in the 1900's also reveals something of the same development. The literary treatment that the Negro received in the fiction of Joel Chandler Harris and George Washington Cable was no doubt often patronizing, sentimentalized, and paternalistic, but there was never anything venomous or bitter about the Negro in their pages.* Rather the total picture that emerges is one that inspires a kind of respect, certainly sympathy, and more often an indulgent tenderness and affection. A stock figure to draw Southern tears was Uncle Remus with the little

* This claim cannot be advanced with the same assurance if extended to Harris' editorial writings, unsigned for the most part, in the Atlanta *Constitution*.

white boy in his lap, or the faithful black retainer of Marse Chan. It is instructive to compare the picture of the Negro painted by these authors who lived through Reconstruction themselves with the picture of the Negro during Reconstruction that emerges in the pages of Thomas Dixon, who was born the last year of the Civil War. Dixon was not of the same caliber as the earlier writers, but he accurately reflects the changed temper of the twentieth-century South. His trilogy: *The Leopard's Spots: A Romance of the White Man's Burden — 1865–1900* (1902) ; *The Clansman: An Historical Romance of the Ku Klux Klan* (1905); and *The Traitor: A Story of the Fall of the Invisible Empire* (1907) was the perfect literary accompaniment of the white-supremacy and disfranchisement campaign, at the height of which they were published.

Scholarship of the period, particularly its sociology, anthropology, and history, likewise reflected the current deterioration in race relations and the new Southern attitudes. Charles Carroll, *'The Negro a Beast'; or, 'In the Image of God'* (1900); William P. Calhoun, *The Caucasian and the Negro in the United States* (1902); William B. Smith, *The Color Line: A Brief in Behalf of the Unborn* (1905); and Robert W. Shufeldt, *The Negro, A Menace to American Civilization* (1907) were a part of the then current national racist literature of the 'Yellow Peril' school and the flourishing cult of Nordicism.

78

Southern historians during the first decade and a half of the century completed the rewriting of Reconstruction history. Their work did not yield completely to the contemporary atmosphere of the white-supremacy movement, but some of it did not entirely escape that influence.

Public-spirited professional people of a humanitarian bent who gathered at periodic conferences to discuss the race problem took a deeply pessimistic or despairing view of the Negro. They laid great stress on the alarming increase in Negro crime as the race flocked to the cities and packed into crowded, filthy slums. They were convinced that the race was rapidly deteriorating in morals and manners, in health and efficiency, and losing out in the struggle for survival. They resolved that the Negro was incapable of self-government, unworthy of the franchise, and impossible to educate beyond the rudiments. They devoted much time and effort to the promotion of Negro education, but the limitations of their aims are indicated by Booker T. Washington when he said in welcoming a conference of white Southern University presidents to Tuskegee in 1912: 'We are trying to instil into the Negro mind that if education does not make the Negro humble, simple, and of service to the community, then it will not be encouraged.'

Professor Paul B. Barringer of the University of Virginia told the Southern Education Association in 1900 that 'The negro race is essentially a race of peasant farmers and laborers . . . As a source of cheap labor for a warm climate he is beyond competition; everywhere else he is a foreordained failure, and as he knows this he despises his own color.' 'Let us go back to the old rule of the South,' urged Barringer, 'and be done forever with the frauds of an educational suffrage.' Southern sentiment in 1904 suggested to Carl Schurz 'a striking resemblance to the pro-slavery arguments . . . heard before the Civil War, and they are brought forth . . . with the same assertion of the negro's predestination for serfdom; the same certainty that he will not work without "physical compulsion"; the same contemptuous rejection of negro education as a thing that will only unfit him for work.'

Wide agreement prevailed in the early years of the century that there was less sympathy, tolerance, and understanding between the races than there had been during the Reconstruction period, and some put the case even more strongly. Professor John Spencer Bassett of Trinity College wrote in 1903 that 'there is today more hatred of whites for blacks and blacks for whites than ever before.' John Temple Graves of Georgia said that 'The races are wider apart, more antagonistic than in 1865.' And the Negro novelist, Charles W. Chesnutt, said in 1903 that 'the rights of the Negroes are at a lower ebb than at any time during the thirty-five years of their

80

freedom, and the race prejudice more intense and uncompromising.'

Such resistance to proscription and segregation as had lingered in the older states of the seaboard South crumbled rapidly. The Richmond *Times* in 1900 demanded that a rigid principle of segregation be 'applied in every relation of Southern life' on the ground that 'God Almighty drew the color line and it cannot be obliterated.' The conservative old Charleston *News and Courier,* quoted at the beginning of this chapter as heaping ridicule upon the Jim Crow movement and the absurdity of its consequences, was of another opinion by 1906. 'The "problem" is worse now than it was ten years ago,' wrote the editor. Far from being ridiculous, segregation did not now seem sufficient. Mass deportation was the remedy. 'Separation of the races is the only radical solution of the negro problem in this country . . . There is no room for them [the Negroes] here,' declared the paper.

5

WITHIN THIS CONTEXT of growing pessimism, mounting tension, and unleashed phobias the structure of segregation and discrimination was extended by the adoption of a great number of the Jim Crow type of laws. Up to 1900 the only law of this type adopted by the majority of Southern states was that applying to passengers aboard trains. And South Carolina did not adopt that until 1898, North Carolina in 1899, and Virginia, the last, in 1900. Only three states had required or authorized the Jim Crow waiting room in railway stations before 1899, but in the next decade nearly all of the other Southern states fell in line. The adoption of laws applying to new subjects tended to take place in waves of popularity. Street cars had been common in Southern cities since the 'eighties, but only Georgia had a segregation law applying to them before the end of the century. Then in quick succession North Carolina and Virginia adopted such a law in 1901, Louisiana in 1902, Arkansas, South Carolina, and Tennessee in 1903, Mississippi and Maryland in 1904, Florida in 1905, and Oklahoma in 1907. These laws referred to separation within cars, but a Montgomery city ordinance of 1906 was the first to require a completely separate Jim Crow street car. During these years the older seaboard states of the South also extended the segregation laws to steamboats.

The mushroom growth of discriminatory and segregation laws during the first two decades of this century piled up a huge bulk of legislation. Much of the code was contributed by city ordinances or by local regulations and rules enforced without the formality of laws. Only a sampling is possible here. For up and down the avenues and byways of Southern life appeared with increasing profusion the little signs: 'Whites Only' or 'Colored.' Sometimes the law prescribed their dimensions in inches, and in one case the kind and color of paint. Many appeared without requirement by law — over entrances and exits, at theaters and boarding houses, toilets and water fountains, waiting rooms and ticket windows.

A large body of law grew up concerned with the segregation of employees and their working conditions. The South Carolina code of 1915, with subsequent elaborations, prohibited textile factories from permitting laborers of different races from working together in the same room, or using the same entrances, pay windows, exits, doorways, stairways, 'or windows [sic]' at the same time, or the same 'lavatories, toilets, drinking water buckets, pails, cups, dippers or glasses' at any time. Exceptions were made of firemen, floor scrubbers, and repair men, who were permitted association with the white proletarian elite on an emergency basis. In most instances segregation in employment was established without the aid of statute. And in many crafts and trades the written or unwritten policies of Jim Crow unionism made segregation superfluous by excluding Negroes from employment.

State institutions for the care of the dependent or incapacitated were naturally the subject of more legislation than private institutions of the same sort, but ordinarily the latter followed pretty closely the segregation practices of the public institutions. The fact that only Mississippi and South Carolina specifically provided for general segregation in hospitals does not indicate that non-segregation was the rule in the hospitals of other states. The two states named also required Negro nurses for Negro patients, and Alabama prohibited white female nurses from attending Negro male patients. Thirteen Southern and border states required the separation of patients by races in mental hospitals, and ten states specified segregation of inmates in penal institutions. Some of the latter went into detail regarding the chaining, transportation, feeding, and working of the prisoners on a segregated basis. Segregation of the races in homes for the aged, the indigent, the orphans, the blind, the deaf, and the dumb is the subject of numerous state laws.

Much ingenuity and effort went into the separation of the races in their amusements, diversions, recreations, and sports. The Separate Park Law of Georgia, adopted in 1905, appears to have been the first venture of a state legislature into this field, though city ordinances and local custom were quite active in pushing the Negro out of the public parks. Circuses and tent shows, including side shows, fell under a law adopted by Louisiana in 1914, which required separate entrances, exits, ticket windows, and ticket sellers that would be kept at least twenty-five feet apart. The city of Birmingham applied the principle to 'any room, hall, theatre, picture house, auditorium, yard, court, ball park, or other indoor or outdoor place' and specified that the races be 'distinctly separated . . . by well defined physical barriers.' North Carolina and Virginia interdicted all fraternal orders or societies that permitted members of both races to address each other as brother.

Residential segregation in cities developed along five different patterns in the second decade of the century. The type originating in Baltimore in 1910 designated all-white and all-Negro blocks in areas occupied by both races. This experiment was imitated in Atlanta and Greenville. Virginia sought to legalize segregation by a state law that authorized city councils to divide territories into segregated districts and to prohibit either race from living in the other's district, a method adopted by Roanoke and Portsmouth, Virginia. The third method, invented by Richmond, designated blocks throughout the city black or white according to the majority of the residents and forbade any person to live in any block 'where the majority of residents on such streets are occupied by those with whom said person is forbidden to intermarry.' This one was later copied by Ashland, Virginia, and Winston-Salem, North Carolina. A still more complicated law originated in Norfolk, which applied to both mixed and unmixed blocks and fixed the color status by ownership as well as occupancy. And finally New Orleans developed a law requiring a person of either race to secure consent of the majority of persons living in an area before establishing a residence therein. After these devices were frustrated by a Supreme Court decision in 1917, attempts continued to be made to circumvent the decision. Probably the most effective of these was the restrictive covenant, a private contract limiting the sale of property in an area to purchasers of the favored race.

The most prevalent and widespread segregation of living areas was accomplished without need for legal sanction. The black ghettos of the 'Darktown' slums in every Southern city were the consequence mainly of the Negro's economic status, his relegation to the lowest rung of the ladder. Smaller towns sometimes excluded Negro residents completely simply by letting it be known in forceful ways that their presence would not be tolerated. In 1914 there were six such towns in Texas, five in Oklahoma, and two in Alabama. On the other hand there were by that time some thirty towns in the South, besides a number of unincorporated settlements, inhabited exclusively by Negroes. In August 1913, Clarence Poe, editor of the *Progressive Farmer,* secured the unanimous endorsement of a convention of the North Carolina Farmer's Union for a movement to segregate the races in rural districts.

The extremes to which caste penalties and separation were carried in parts of the South could hardly find a counterpart short of the latitudes of India and South Africa. In 1909 Mobile passed a curfew law applying exclusively to Negroes and requiring them to be off the streets by 10 p.m. The Oklahoma legislature in 1915 authorized its Corporation Commission to require telephone companies 'to maintain separate booths for white and colored patrons.' North Carolina and Florida required that textbooks used by the public-school children of one race be kept separate from those used by the other, and the Florida law specified separation even while the books were in storage. South Carolina for a time segregated a third caste by establishing separate schools for mulatto as well as for white and Negro children. A New Orleans ordinance segregated white and Negro prostitutes in separate districts. Ray Stannard Baker found Jim Crow Bibles for Negro witnesses in Atlanta courts and Jim Crow elevators for Negro passengers in Atlanta buildings.

6

A SEARCH of the statute books fails to disclose any state law or city ordinance specifying separate Bibles and separate elevators. Right here it is well to admit, and even to emphasize, that laws are not an adequate index of the extent and prevalence of segregation and discriminatory practices in the South. The practices often anticipated and sometimes exceeded the laws. It may be confidently assumed — and it could be verified by present observation — that there is more Jim Crowism practiced in the South than there are Jim Crow laws on the books.

87

To say that, however, is not to concede the position so often taken by Southern as well as Northern writers that the laws were of little consequence anyway. This view consciously or unconsciously voices a laissez-faire bias and often leans for support upon the authority of William Graham Sumner. It was the contention of Sumner's classic *Folkways*, published in 1907, that 'legislation cannot make mores' and that 'stateways cannot change folkways.' Sumner described these 'folkways' as 'uniform, universal in the group, imperative, and invariable.' Perhaps it was not his intention, but Sumner's teachings lent credence to the existence of a primeval rock of human nature upon which the waves of legislation beat in vain. This concept as it was applied to Southern race practices and caste penalties was further buttressed by an American apostle of Herbert Spencer, the sociologist Franklin Henry Giddings. His emphasis upon 'consciousness of kind' in works appearing in 1896 and the decade following gave aid and comfort to the followers of Sumner. So did the racist interpretations of the psychologist William McDougall, whose *Introduction to Social Psychology* appeared in 1908.

Since the works mentioned represented the dominant American social theory of the early twentieth century, and since they appeared in the years when the wave of Southern and American racism was reaching its crest, it was natural that they should have influenced thinking upon the South's major social preoccupation. Their influence was to encourage the notion that there was something inevitable and rigidly inflexible about the existing patterns of segregation and race relations in the South; that these patterns had not been and could not be altered by conscious effort; and that it was, indeed, folly to attempt to meddle with them by means of legislation. These early twentieth-century theories have been characterized by a present-day psychologist, Kenneth B. Clark, as 'the modern attempt at acceptable restatement of the medieval doctrine of *innate ideas.*' Conceived of as biological or social imperatives, these modern 'innate ideas' were presented as 'folkways' or 'mores' which explained and, by inference, justified the existing structure of society, the privileges and policies of the dominant race, and the subordination of the minority race.

This body of social theory, though outmoded by later discovery, continued to be pressed into use for various purposes down to quite recent times. Thus David L. Cohn wrote in the *Atlantic Monthly* of January 1944, 'It is William Graham Sumner's dictum that you cannot change the mores of a people by law, and since the social segregation of the races is the most deep-seated and pervasive of the Southern mores, it is evident that he who attempts to change it by law runs risks of incalculable gravity.' Among such risks he cited 'civil war' as one.

There was a curious contradiction or inconsistency implicit in the theory of this school in so far as it was applied to the history of race relations in the South. When William Graham Sumner wrote that 'The whites [in the South] have never been converted from the old mores' and that 'Vain attempts have been made to control the new order by legislation,' he was thinking of the legislative efforts of radical Reconstruction. Those were the laws he had in mind when he said that 'The only result is the proof that legislation cannot make mores.' It was the same experiment that the historian William H. Dunning, Giddings' colleague at Columbia, referred to in saying, 'The enfranchisement of the freedman was as reckless a species of statecraft, as that which marked "the blind hysterics of the Celt" in 1789–95.' And yet Southerners cited these authorities upon the utter futility of legislation in the alteration of relations between races to justify and support an elaborate program of legislation to change the relations between races in a different direction. The inference would seem to be that while sound scientific theory proved that folkways and mores could not be changed for some purposes, it proved at the same time that they could be changed for other purposes.

At any rate, the findings of the present investigation tend to bear out the testimony of Negroes from various parts of the South, as reported by the Swedish writer Gunnar Myrdal, to the effect that 'the Jim Crow statutes were effective means of tightening and freezing — in many cases instigating — segregation and discrimination.' The evidence has indicated that under conditions prevailing in the earlier part of the period reviewed the Negro could and did do many things in the South that in the latter part of the period, under different conditions, he was prevented from doing.

We have seen that in the 'seventies, 'eighties, and 'nineties the Negroes voted in large numbers. White leaders of opposing parties encouraged them to vote and earnestly solicited their votes. Qualified and acknowledged leaders of Southern white opinion were on record as saying that it was proper, inevitable, and desirable that they should vote. Yet after the disfranchisement measures were passed around 1900 the Negroes ceased to vote. And at that time qualified and acknowledged leaders of white opinion said that it was unthinkable that they should ever be permitted to vote. In the earlier decades Negroes still took an active, if modest, part in public life. They held offices, served on the jury, the bench, and were represented in local councils, state legislatures, and the national Congress. Later on these things were simply not so, and the last of the Negroes disappeared from these forums.

It has also been seen that their presence on trains upon equal terms with white men was once re-

91

garded as normal, acceptable, and unobjectionable. Whether railways qualify as folkways or stateways, black man and white man once rode them together and without a partition between them. Later on the stateways apparently changed the folkways — or at any rate the railways — for the partitions and Jim Crow cars became universal. And the new seating arrangement came to seem as normal, unchangeable, and inevitable as the old ways. And so it was with the soda fountains, eating places, bars, waiting rooms, street cars, and circuses. And so it probably was with the parks in Atlanta, and with cemeteries in Mississippi. There must even have been a time in Oklahoma when a colored man could walk into any old telephone booth he took a notion to and pick up the receiver.

What was once said in extenuation of the harshness of the black codes of slavery times — that they were more honored in the breach than in the observance — cannot be said of the Jim Crow codes. Any Southerner of middle age, of course, could think of exceptions: the old 'auntie' who came to talk with one's grandmother on Saturday afternoons when the weather was nice; the privileged 'uncle' who preferred and was permitted to attend the white church; the defiant 'mammy' on the white day coach; and the old retainer who lorded it over the family larder and put the grocer's white delivery boy in his place. But we recognize them all as belated survivors of the old times — relics now gone with the second wind of history.

Barring those disappearing exceptions, the Jim Crow laws applied to *all* Negroes — not merely to the rowdy, or drunken, or surly, or ignorant ones. The new laws did not countenance the old conservative tendency to distinguish between classes of the race, to encourage the 'better' element, and to draw it into a white alliance. Those laws backed up the Alabamian who told the disfranchising convention of his state that no Negro in the world was the equal of 'the least, poorest, lowest-down white man I ever knew'; but not ex-Governor Oates, who replied: 'I would not trust him as quickly as I would a negro of intelligence and good character.' The Jim Crow laws put the authority of the state or city in the voice of the street-car conductor, the railway brakeman, the bus driver, the theater usher, and also into the voice of the hoodlum of the public parks and playgrounds. They gave free rein and the majesty of the law to mass aggressions that might otherwise have been curbed, blunted, or deflected.

The Jim Crow laws, unlike feudal laws, did not assign the subordinate group a fixed status in society. They were constantly pushing the Negro farther down. In seeking to distinguish between the Southern white attitudes toward the Negro during Reconstruction and the era following and the attitudes later developed, Edgar Gardner Murphy in

1911 called the one 'defensive' and 'conservative' and the other 'increasingly aggressive' and 'destructive.' 'The new mood,' he wrote, 'makes few professions of conservatism. It does not claim to be necessary to the state's existence . . . These new antipathies are not defensive, but assertive and combative . . . frankly and ruthlessly destructive.' The movement had proceeded in mounting stages of aggression. 'Its spirit is that of an all-absorbing autocracy of race, an animus of aggrandizement which makes, in the imagination of the white man, an absolute identification of the stronger race with the very being of the state.'

We have come a long way since that time and since that mood prevailed in the South. But most of the distance we have traveled has been covered in very recent years. The most common observation upon recent developments in race relations by intelligent white people of the South is almost invariably prefaced by the phrase: 'Ten years ago I would never have believed that . . .' And, indeed, ten years ago there was little reason to believe, or to expect that things would change in the South at any more than a glacial pace. For as recently as that the doctrine according to Sumner prevailed almost unchallenged in the mind of the laity — as well as in the minds of a good part of the 'experts' on social problems. And that doctrine had it that however crying the need was for change, those immovable 'folkways' and irresistible 'mores' made the whole idea impracticable, or slowed down change to the pace of evolution.

When a scientific theory ceases to account for the observed facts of common experience, however, it would seem to be time to discard the theory. In lieu of another to offer in its place, we can at least try to understand what has happened.

III / The Man on the Cliff

IN THE SECOND YEAR of the First World War, Maurice S. Evans, an Englishman who made his home in South Africa, wrote a book on race relations in the South that, according to the subtitle, was written 'From a South African Point of View.' He found conditions in the South 'strikingly similar' to those he had left behind at home. 'The separation of the races in all social matters,' he wrote, 'is as distinct in South Africa as in the Southern States. There are separate railway cars . . . and no black man enters hotel, theatre, public library or art gallery.' There were also in his homeland the same separate schools, the same disfranchisement, and the same political and economic subordination of the black man. 'How often,' he exclaimed, 'the very conditions I had left were reproduced before my eyes, the thousands of miles melted away, and Africa was before me.' Evans thought that 'in essence the problem is the same for both of us' — South Africa and the Southern states of America — and that the two great regions should and probably would pursue much the same course toward the solution of their common problems in the future. He particularly urged upon the South 'a separation of the races such as is still possible to us in South Africa,' where 'we still have the black States.' He believed that this solution would be worth 'heavy sacrifices to ensure it.'

At the time of the First World War there was much to lend plausibility to Evans' prediction that the South and South Africa would follow parallel courses in the future. And there was at that time little evidence to indicate that their paths would eventually come to a point of sharp divergence. Thoughtful Southerners such as Alfred H. Stone, a planter from the Yazoo delta of Mississippi, were conscious of the parallel between the policies pursued by the dominant whites of the two regions. 'There are more Negroes in Mississippi,' wrote Stone, 'than in Cape Colony, or Natal, even with the great territory of Zululand annexed to the latter; more than in the Transvaal, and not far from as many as in both the Boer colonies combined.' He remarked that the movement for disfranchisement had been 'simultaneously agitated in both Cape

Colony and Mississippi,' and that action on the subject in the colony had followed hard upon that in his state, with an interval of only two years between them.

1

THERE WAS AS YET no sign of a revival of Northern resistance to Southern race policy. If anything, thought Thomas P. Bailey, Northern opposition was still on the decline. In his *Race Orthodoxy in the South,* published in 1914, Bailey asked: 'Is not the South being *encouraged* to treat the negroes *as aliens* by the growing discrimination against the negro in the North, a discrimination that is social as well as economic? Does not the South perceive that all the fire has gone out of the Northern philanthropic fight for the rights of man? *The North has surrendered!'* According to Bailey it was 'the underlying feeling of many a Southern leader' that ' "They are going to let us alone; we'll fix things to suit ourselves." ' The trend in the North, he believed, was toward the adoption of the Southern Way as the American Way. 'Even now,' he observed, 'the solid Far West is joining hands with the South in racial matters; and the end is not yet in the growing solidarity of the white people in this country.'

The concentration upon the South as the arbitrarily limited subject of these lectures should not lead to the inference that the attitudes and policies described here were peculiar to the South. Indeed, if there were time and space, it would be a simple matter to point out the many parallel lines of prejudice and discrimination against the Negro in the North, prejudice that often worked as great a hardship upon the race as it did in the South. The trend toward racism in the North was amply illustrated in the years immediately following the First World War.

The war aroused in the Negroes a new hope for restoration of their rights and a new militancy in demanding first-class citizenship. More than 360,000 of them entered military service and a large part of those saw overseas duty in uniform. More joined the exodus of migration to the North in quest of high wages in the war industries. Temporary prosperity gave them new hopes and desires that needed fulfillment, and official propaganda picturing American participation in the war as a crusade for democracy raised the natural demand for a little more democracy at home.

The war-bred hopes of the Negro for first-class citizenship were quickly smashed in a reaction of violence that was probably unprecedented. Some twenty-five race riots were touched off in American cities during the last six months of 1919, months that John Hope Franklin called 'the greatest period of interracial strife the nation had ever witnessed.' Mobs took over cities for days at a time, flogging, burning, shooting, and torturing at will. When the

Negroes showed a new disposition to fight and defend themselves, violence increased. Some of these atrocities occurred in the South — at Longview, Texas, for example, or at Tulsa, Oklahoma, at Elaine, Arkansas, or Knoxville, Tennessee. But they were limited to no one section of the country. Many of them occurred in the North and the worst of all in Chicago. During the first year following the war more than seventy Negroes were lynched, several of them veterans still in uniform.

In the postwar era there were new indications that the Southern Way was spreading as the American Way in race relations. The great migration of Negroes into the residential slum areas and the industrial plants of the big Northern cities increased tension between races. Northern labor was jealous of its status and resentful of the competition of Negroes, who were excluded from unions. Negroes were pushed out of the more desirable jobs in industries that they had succeeded in invading during the manpower shortage of the war years. They were squeezed out of federal employment more and more. Negro postmen began to disappear from their old routes, as they did from the police beats. They began to lose their grip upon crafts such as that of the barbers, which had once been a virtual monopoly in the South.

Racism in regimented form was spread over the whole country in the 'twenties by the new Ku Klux

Klan. Organized in Georgia in 1915, the new Klan did not reach its peak of membership, reported to have been five million, until the mid-twenties. Directed against other racial and religious minorities, as well as against the Negro, the Klan attained a larger following outside the South than within. Its influence within the South, however, toward the inflaming of prejudice, the encouragement of race violence, and the strengthening of the segregation code was powerful. At least two state governments, those of Texas and Oklahoma, were for a time almost completely under the domination of the Klan. Though the formal organization declined rapidly before the end of the 'twenties, sporadic outbreaks of its activities continued in the lower South into the 'fifties.

There was no apparent tendency toward abatement or relaxation of the Jim Crow code of discrimination and segregation in the 1920's, and none in the 'thirties until well along in the depression years. In fact the Jim Crow laws were elaborated and further expanded in those years. Much social and economic history is reflected in the new laws. When women began to bob their hair and become patrons of the barber shops, Atlanta passed an ordinance in 1926 forbidding Negro barbers to serve women or children under fourteen years of age. Jim Crow kept step with the march of progress in transportation and industry, as well as with the changes in fashion.

102

Mississippi brought her transportation laws abreast of the times in 1922 by passing a state-wide Jim Crow law applying to taxicabs. City ordinances requiring Jim Crow taxis were adopted by Jacksonville in 1929, by Birmingham in 1930, and by Atlanta in 1940. The Atlanta law required signs 'in an oil paint of contrasting color' painted on the vehicle to indicate which race it served, and further specified that 'There shall be white drivers for carrying white passengers and colored drivers for carrying colored passengers.' The advent of the cross-country buses as serious competitors of the railways was marked by the extension of the Jim Crow train law to the buses in all particulars, including seating arrangement, waiting rooms, toilets, and other accommodations. The arrival of the age of air transportation appears to have put a strain upon the ingenuity of the Jim Crow lawmakers. Even to the orthodox there was doubtless something slightly incongruous about requiring a Jim Crow compartment on a Lockheed Constellation or a DC-6, particularly one that touched the ground only once between Washington and Miami. No Jim Crow law has been found that applies to passengers while they are in the air. So long as they were upon the ground, however, they were still subject to Jim Crow jurisdiction. The Virginia legislature empowered the State Corporation Commission in 1944 to require separate waiting rooms and other facilities in airports. Air companies generally complied with custom without the compulsion of law — at least so far as activities on the ground were concerned.

In the field of recreation, sports, and amusements the laws continued to be tightened. An Atlanta ordinance of June 1940 made the single exception of its park segregation 'so much of Grant park as is occupied by the zoo.' Only in the presence of the lower anthropoids could law-abiding Atlantans of different races consort together. The same city in 1932 prohibited amateur baseball clubs of different races from playing within two blocks of each other. In 1933 Texas prohibited 'Caucasians' and 'Africans' from boxing and wrestling together. Federal law stepped in to hinder the circulation of films showing interracial boxing. An Arkansas law of 1937 required segregation at all race tracks and gaming establishments 'in seating, betting, and all other accommodations.' In 1935 Oklahoma extended the white man's law to separate the races while fishing or boating. A Birmingham ordinance got down to particulars in 1930 by making it 'unlawful for a Negro and a white person to play together or in company with each other' at dominoes or checkers.

By 1944 the Swedish writer Gunnar Myrdal observed that 'Segregation is now becoming so complete that the white Southerner practically never sees a Negro except as his servant and in other standardized and formalized caste situations.'

104

2

TENSION BETWEEN THE RACES eased somewhat during the 'thirties while both white and colored people grappled with the problems of the Great Depression. For the first time in history the great majority of both races in the South joined the same political party. Under a liberal administration that party appeared to be sincerely striving to improve the lot of the black man as well as that of the white man. In spite of unyielding segregation, a few new opportunities opened to the Negro in cultural life, housing, health improvement, and education through federal agencies of the New Deal. Interracial violence, particularly lynching, declined markedly. Southern white people and even the liberals among them were beginning to congratulate themselves upon the dawn of what seemed to be a new and hopeful era of interracial relations.

Then, quite abruptly and unaccountably — or so it seemed to many Southern white people — an avalanche of denunciation, criticism, and opprobrium descended upon the South from above the Mason and Dixon line. Militant and organized demands from both Negro and white sources of pressure were raised for immediate abolition of segregation. There was a harsh intolerance and aggressiveness about the new agitation that frightened the South. Coming on the heels of what some Southerners had considered a period of progress in racial

105

relations, the demands seemed the more unreasonable and unfair. They coincided with the war crisis that had already frayed people's nerves. It was sometimes hard to tell whether the international or the interracial conflict excited the bitterest feeling. Howard W. Odum in his *Race and Rumors of Race* has vividly described the atmosphere of suspicion and fear that brooded over the South in the early 'forties. The flying rumors of plot and counterplot, of bands armed with icepick and switch-blade knife, of Eleanor Clubs, conspiratorial societies, and subversive Northern agitators often recall the fevered frame of mind that possessed the South in the winter following the Harpers Ferry raid. To the experienced sociologist Odum, it seemed that 'the South and the Negro in the early 1940's, faced their greatest crisis since the days of the reconstruction and that many of the same symbols of conflict and tragedy that were manifest in the 1840's were evident again a hundred years later.'

Responsible and liberal-minded spokesmen of the South, gravely alarmed, felt it necessary to issue stern warnings. 'A small group of Negro agitators and another small group of white rabble-rousers,' wrote Virginius Dabney in January 1943, 'are pushing this country closer and closer to an interracial explosion which may make the race riots of the First World War and its aftermath seem mild by comparison. Unless saner counsels prevail, we may have the worst internal clashes since Reconstruction, with hundreds, if not thousands, killed and amicable race relations set back for decades.' Other writers invoked the Sumnerian imperative of the incorrigible folkways to stem the tide of agitation. 'A fact as sure as science,' declared John Temple Graves, 'is that the white majorities of the South are unwavering and total in their determination not to have race segregation abolished.' According to David L. Cohn, 'Southern whites, therefore, will not at any foreseeable time relax the taboos and conventions which keep the races separate, from the cradle to the grave.' And in the words of Mark Ethridge, 'There is no power in the world — not even in all the mechanized armies of the earth, Allied and Axis — which could now force Southern white people to the abandonment of the principle of social segregation.'

With the advantage of hindsight that these gentlemen did not enjoy, we now know that things did not turn out in quite the way these pessimistic utterances predicted. The interracial explosion that would have made the riots following the First World War mild by comparison fortunately did not materialize. And furthermore, despite the Sumnerian imperative, the incorrigible taboos and mores have in the meantime relaxed perceptibly at several points between the cradle and the grave. In fact, the point that was a decade ago so confidently pro-

107

claimed to be the *ne plus ultra* of Southern tolerance actually marked the beginning of the period of most rapid advance against the walls of segregation that has yet been made — an advance that does not yet appear to have been halted.

At some point along their parallel ways it is now clear that the paths of the South and of South Africa diverged. At the time of the First World War it had seemed that both regions were going roughly the same way. But by the time the Second World War was over it was very plain that they were no longer traveling together. Indeed, as the tragic destination of South Africa became more and more apparent, and as more hopeful events transpired on the other side of the Atlantic, it began to seem as if the two great regions might be traveling in opposite directions. Historians will long dispute the turning point of the South and the reasons for the momentous change of course. The first who attempt to plot the course and explain the change will make mistakes in emphasis and interpretation that will probably seem ludicrous to those who will later have the advantage of hindsight and perspective. But someone has to make a beginning.

3

FOR ALMOST A CENTURY NOW historians have disputed the decisive factors that led to the first era of emancipation and Reconstruction. To some it has seemed that ideas and their propagation and dissemination have been the important influences. Such historians have naturally stressed the roles of the agitator, the propagandist, and the pressure group. They have dwelt at length upon the abolitionist crusade and the various anti-slavery leaders — their societies, tactics, and the influence these have had upon the course of events. Other writers have deprecated the importance of such influences and have instead laid greater stress upon impersonal, amoral, and non-volitional forces of history. Such people have emphasized the part played by conflicting commercial, industrial, and financial interests of large groups, the blind surges of mass emotions, the exigencies of party politics, and the harsh expedients of modern warfare. No really capable historian has entirely neglected any of these forces, and the better of them have attempted syntheses of all. But they have so far not arrived at a consensus that has met with anything approaching general endorsement.

All the various forces, moral and amoral, whose importance the historians have disputed in explaining the first era of emancipation and Reconstruction have their counterparts in the historical background of the movement we are presently attempting to understand. For the modern development also has a background of ideas, propaganda, agitation, and pressure groups as well as a background of conflicting economic interests, power politics, and war. In both the nineteenth-century and the twentieth-century movements, emotional factors of race prejudice and sectional pride, as well as the compulsions of frustration and aggression, have played their parts. It will long be a matter of debate as to the relative importance played by the agitators, foreign and domestic propaganda, the courts, the White House, party politics, two or three wars, post-war prosperity, the seemingly interminable Cold War, or the dubious influence of nationalism and oppressive conformity working in a new direction. It would be foolhardy to attempt, with no more than the foreshortened and distorting perspective we now have, to arrive at anything more than a very tentative assessment of the bewilderingly complex forces involved and the relative importance of the part each has played.

The evaluation of ideas and their agitation is most difficult because of the impossibility of measuring the results. It is clear at least that the Negro himself played a larger role in the new movement for emancipation than he had in the abolitionist crusade that led to the original emancipation. There were peripheral and lunatic-fringe movements such as those led by Marcus Garvey and 'Father Divine,' but the majority of the more responsible and intelligent of the Negro agitators identified themselves with such organizations as the National Association for the Advancement of Colored People. An interracial organization founded in 1909, the N.A.A.C.P. performed effective work in agitating against discrimination and lynching, but gained no mass support or powerful influence for the first decade or more. Between the First and Second World Wars, however, the number of local chapters increased from about fifty to more than ten times that number. Claiming a membership of half a million, the association became a power to be reckoned with in national politics. In the meantime the National Urban League had been established in forty-eight cities, and the National Negro Congress, another civil-rights group, had organized more than a hundred chapters. These organizations attracted powerful support from the white world, without which they could never have achieved what they did.

Of great importance in arousing the sympathy and stimulating the support of white intellectuals and philanthropists was the Negro literary and artistic awakening of the 'twenties and 'thirties sometimes called the 'Harlem Renaissance.' A sudden outpouring of formidable proportions, some of it good and some bad, the Negro fiction, poetry, and song was highly race-conscious and inspired by the spirit of protest. New poets and novelists gained national attention by giving voice to the ancient wrongs, the brooding sorrows, and the mounting indignation of their race. White admirers patronized and encouraged their efforts with publicity and funds. Negro art for a time enjoyed an enormous vogue, and the Negro himself acquired a prestige as a *cause célèbre* among intellectuals and the philanthropically inclined, a prestige second only to that of the proletariat in the 'thirties. When the proletariat became more prosperous and less fashionable, the Negro remained the residuary repository of thwarted humanitarianism.

Religious sentiment is not to be neglected in the briefest sketch of the agitation for Negro rights. The 'social gospel' movement began to permeate the great Protestant sects in the early years of the century. As the breach between the estranged Northern and Southern branches of Methodism and the other churches healed more firmly in the 'thirties, the Northern extension of the social gospel to include the Negro and his wrongs made itself felt in the Southern connections as well. The more solidly organized Roman Catholics simultaneously moved in the same direction. By the 1940's some of the most advanced pronouncements to be heard in the South were coming from religious sources.

The American faith in equality of opportunity and equality of rights has never really known any sectional boundaries. It has been professed as devoutly in the South as elsewhere, even by those who know their racial views are inconsistent with the national faith and acknowledge that the status ac-

112

corded the Negro represents a lag in public morals. It has been the avowed mission of Southern liberals to sting the conscience of the South into an intensified awareness of the inconsistency between creed and custom. By the third decade of the twentieth century there had grown up in the South a considerable body of indigenous urban liberal strength that was gaining important influence. Avowed liberals for the first time in our history began to direct the editorial policies of some of the oldest and strongest Southern newspapers. Southern liberals also began to appear in the highest political offices, on the floor of the Senate, on the Supreme Court bench, and in advisory offices close to the White House.

One of the earliest vehicles of liberal influence in the South was the Commission on Interracial Cooperation, organized in 1919, 'to quench, if possible, the fires of racial antagonism which were flaming at that time.' Moderate in tone, the commission emphasized an educational program and directed its attack against lynching and discrimination, but not segregation. The tradition established by the commission has been ably promoted by its successor, the Southern Regional Council, founded in 1944. More militant and radical than either of these was the Southern Conference for Human Welfare, which was launched in 1938 with an aggressive program in behalf of all underprivileged groups. Chief among

113

these groups was, naturally, the Negro, and the demands made in his behalf were not limited by the same deference to prevailing opinion that earlier Southern agitators had shown.

The twentieth-century crusade for Negro rights began about as long before the practical politicians took it up as did the nineteenth-century abolitionist crusade. But unlike the abolitionists, whose fervor reached its climax more than two decades before their program achieved practical consummation, the modern crusaders have sustained a mounting crescendo of enthusiasm and pressure. The flood of anti-slavery petitions and bills that reached its crest and all but stopped the wheels of Congress in the early 1840's had subsided to a trickle in the 1850's. On the other hand, in the recent period, while only ten bills favorable to civil rights were introduced in the Seventy-fifth Congress (1937–8), the number of such bills increased in each succeeding Congress until in the Eighty-first Congress (1949–50) seventy-two were introduced.

It is evident from many other indications that before this time the practical politicians and strategists of the two great political parties were vitally interested in a movement that agitators and propagandists had started. To understand why this happened, just as to understand why abolitionism became involved in practical politics, we must turn

114

from the realm of ideas, moral principles, and their agitators to the sphere of the more amoral and impersonal forces.

Several of these forces have enormously swelled the great migration of Negroes from the South in recent years. In the decade of the 'forties alone the number of Negroes living outside the South jumped from 2,360,000 to 4,600,000, an increase of nearly 100 per cent. At the present time considerably more than one-third of the Negroes in the country live outside of the South, as compared with about one-tenth fifty years ago. Most of this increase has gone to the industrial states, where the Negro population has increased from five to ten times as fast as the white between 1940 and 1950. Within the South in that same decade, on the other hand, the white-population increase proved to be thirty-three times as great as the gain in the number of Negroes. What the South has long claimed as its peculiar problem is no longer a regional monopoly, but is increasingly a national problem.

These population changes have had many implications for the changes in the Negro's status and the movement for his rights. The Northern Negro population is largely urban and the Southern Negroes are increasingly so. The importance of civil rights and the laws that define and protect them increases for the Negro in proportion to his urbanization.

His power for making effective political demand for his rights has also increased as he has moved northward and cityward.

The shift in Negro population has had far-reaching political implications, for the Negroes outside the South were located mainly in closely contested urban centers and industrial states. But instead of dividing their votes between the two great parties and becoming, as their leaders hoped, a 'balance of power' that would compel both parties to bid for their support, the Negroes have flocked fairly solidly to the Democratic standard and cast off their historic allegiance to the Republican party. The result has been something like a complete reversal of the traditional position of the two major parties toward the Negro, as a survey of the 1948 and 1952 elections would clearly indicate. The party of white supremacy had become on the national plane the outspoken champion of Negro rights, while the party of emancipation had been left free to seek alliance in the South with the disaffected white-supremacy leaders. At the same time the strategic location of the Negro minority in the North had made it sometimes more important to the success of the Democratic party in national elections than the disaffected whites in the Southern wing of the Democracy. The effect of this reversal had been unmistakably registered in the national Democratic platforms of the last decade as well as in the domestic

116

policies and pronouncements of President Franklin
D. Roosevelt and President Harry S. Truman.

Specific instances of the preponderant influence
of the Northern Negro minority over Democratic
administrations as compared with Southern influence are seen in President Roosevelt's directive, in
1941, creating a federal Committee on Fair Employment Practices; and in President Truman's appointment in 1946 of a Commission on Higher
Education and a Committee on Civil Rights. Roosevelt's F.E.P.C. grew out of the crisis in shortage of
labor during the war, but the directive establishing
the committee was exacted from the President by
determined and aggressive pressure of Negro civil-
rights organizations. Truman's Commission on
Higher Education condemned inequality of opportunity on account of color and race and concluded
in its report of 1947 that 'there will be no funda-
mental correction of the total condition until segregation legislation is repealed.' The uncompromising report of the President's Committee on Civil
Rights, entitled *To Secure These Rights,* urged the
'elimination of segregation, based on race, color,
creed, or national origin, from American life.' In
the face of a revolt that eventually took four states
of the lower South out of his party, President Truman, in February 1948, urged the enactment of an
F.E.P.C. law, the outlawing of poll tax and lynching, the elimination of segregation in interstate

117

transportation, a law to enforce fairness in elections, and the establishment of a permanent civil-rights commission. In the same year Truman issued an executive order directing the elimination of discrimination in federal employment, and another momentous order to end segregation in the armed services.

In spite of the prosperity boom of the war and postwar years which has scattered wealth so profusely, the great majority of lower-class Negroes probably still live close to the subsistence level of existence. An urban middle class of the race, however, has benefited by a share of the prosperity and has entered the competitive struggle to achieve and maintain middle-class living standards and climb up in the world. Rather sharply differentiated from the lower class of the race, the Negro middle class has made a strong bid for the respect and deference of the white world. This bid was registered in dress and speech, in consumer habits, as well as in conduct. Such courtesy and deference as they have won may have been in considerable measure inspired by competition for the increased purchasing power of the Negro, but that has not been the only source. These people have begun to produce talent in the arts, in academic life, and in politics that has done much to reinforce their claim to a rise in status. Another effect of the prosperity boom has been that the South has begun to pull out of its seventy-five-year

118

stalemate of an underprivileged and colonial econ-
omy. In the process the South has begun to find
that it is easier to share prosperity than poverty with
the minority race.

War and international tension, as well as the
business cycle, have made their impact felt upon the
pattern of racial relations in the South. The foremost of the Axis powers against which the United
States fought in the Second World War was the most
forceful exponent of racism the modern world has
known. The Nazi crime against the minority race,
more than anything else, was the offense against the
Western moral code that branded the Reich as an
outlaw power. Adolph Hitler's doctrine of the 'master race' had as its chief victim the Jew, but the
association of that doctrine with the creed of white
supremacy was inevitably made in the American
mind. That association is not likely to be broken
very easily. American war propaganda stressed
above all else the abhorrence of the West for Hitler's brand of racism and its utter incompatibility
with the democratic faith for which we fought. The
relevance of this deep stirring of the American conscience for the position of the Negro was not lost
upon him and his champions. Awareness of the inconsistency between practice at home and propaganda abroad placed a powerful lever in their
hands.

Almost as soon as the crusade against Hitler and

119

the Axis powers was concluded, we found ourselves locked in the grip of a Cold War with a former ally. Communist propaganda had long used stories of racial discrimination and injustice to discredit American capitalism and democracy in the eyes of the world. This issue gained tremendously in poignancy when the two powers faced each other in an ideological struggle for world leadership. It came near the focus of antagonism when the center of rivalry between Russia and America shifted to Asia and the two systems began to contend desperately for the friendship of the great colored races of the Orient. In this struggle the issue of segregation, far from being confined to regional boundaries, became international in scope. The daily press of Tokyo, Delhi, Peiping, and Saigon was diligently searched in our State Department for reactions to the latest outburst of interracial violence in Florida or Detroit, or the latest Supreme Court decision on segregation.

In a brief filed in December 1952 with the Supreme Court in connection with the cases involving segregation in the public schools, the Democratic United States Attorney General said: 'It is in the context of the present world struggle between freedom and tyranny that the problem of racial discrimination must be viewed . . . Racial discrimination furnishes grist for the Communist propaganda mills, and it raises doubt even among friendly na-

120

tions as to the intensity of our devotion to the democratic faith.' He quoted the Secretary of State in his brief as saying: 'The segregation of school children on a racial basis is one of the practices in the United States which has been singled out for hostile foreign comment in the United Nations and elsewhere. Other peoples cannot understand how such a practice can exist in a country which professes to be a staunch supporter of freedom, justice, and democracy.' Within a few hours after the Supreme Court's decision was read in 1954, the Voice of America had broadcast the news to foreign countries in thirty-five separate languages.

The establishment of the United Nations and the bringing of the headquarters of the organization to these shores suddenly threw open to the outside world a large window on American race practices. Through that window soon gazed a passing stream of delegates from all nations and races of the earth. To many of these people the Jim Crow code came as a complete shock. Those who had heard anything at all of the system before coming to America often discounted the stories as propaganda. Now they witnessed its workings daily. More important still were the United Nations committees of investigation, their numerous published reports, and the public debates that dealt with racial discrimination and injustice. The publicity thus focused upon this weak joint in America's moral armor caused genu-

121

ine and practical embarrassment to the State Department in the conduct of foreign affairs. One of several stratagems employed to recover lost ground has been the appointment of numbers of Negroes to posts in the Foreign Service of the Department. Some of these posts have been of high rank and importance and have opened to Negroes a new access to prestige hitherto unattainable for them. National pride in the achievements of Ralph Bunche as an American spokesman illustrates the effect that the new prominence of the Negro in this field can have upon old prejudices and stereotypes.

There was concern in high office not only for the struggle over the allegiance of colored peoples in foreign lands but also for the allegiance of our own colored people at home. This was especially true with regard to the Negro intellectuals and the Negro labor leaders. Communist propaganda made a strong, powerfully organized, and concerted — if somewhat blundering — drive to alienate the Negro from his faith in American institutions, to destroy his hope for justice under segregation, and to win over his allegiance to the revolutionary cause. The effect this campaign had may be detected in the Negro periodicals, literature, and pronouncements of the 'thirties and 'forties, as well as among Negro leaders in cultural, intellectual, and labor fields. That the Communists failed was due only in part to their blundering. It was also due to a counter drive to revive the Negro's hope for a larger share in American democracy.

The decade and a half of World War and Cold War has bred in this country a new temper of intense nationalism. One manifestation of this spirit has been a blind passion for stamping out subversion of all sorts, and in its blindness that passion has struck out at nonconformity in almost any form. The heedless demand for conformity has placed civil rights and traditional freedom of thought and expression in greater jeopardy than ever before in our history. There are those who find some comfort in the progress that has been made during the last decade in leveling the barriers of discrimination and segregation that have blocked the civil rights of the Negro. Such people point out hopefully that these advances have paradoxically coincided with the peak of reactionism. It is hard to begrudge anyone a crumb of comfort in times such as these. But the ironic reflection is unavoidable that desegregation — whether a subject of rejoicing or not — is itself in part a by-product of the very wave of nationalism and conformity that is so justly deplored.

The chief agent for the advance against Southern peculiarities of racial discrimination and segregation has been the federal government in its several branches and departments, both civil and military. The advances in leveling some of the distinctive barriers in Southern states could never have come so rapidly and effectively had not the powers and functions of the federal government undergone an unprecedented expansion during the last two decades. This expansion has been felt not only as an increase in power but also as an extension of that power into relations of employment, welfare, education, housing, and travel, where it had never before penetrated. In part the result of the crisis of the Great Depression, the enlargement of government functions and power was also a product of the same forces that have produced the oppressive wave of conformity — international tension, intensified nationalism, and war, both hot and cold.

4

THE ATTACK upon the old system of disfranchisement and segregation has scored so many gains in the last decade that it is impossible to give anything approaching a complete account of them here. Only a sketch of the more significant ones will be attempted. Taken together, however, they represent a range and rapidity of alteration in racial relations of the South that might be not inappropriately called a 'New Reconstruction.'

The return of the Negro to the polls of the South after virtual exclusion for nearly half a century is surely one of the more significant aspects of this New Reconstruction. Persistent efforts to abolish the poll tax by federal law have so far been defeated by filibuster tactics in the Senate, but the states themselves have been taking action against this barrier to the ballot with the result that only five Southern states still retain the tax. Poll-tax, property, and literacy qualifications for suffrage, as a matter of fact, have been declining as effective restraints upon Negro voters as economic and educational standards have improved. The final, and most formidable, barrier to the polls was the white primary, and that was toppled by a series of federal court decisions. Beginning in 1941 with the *Classic* case, the United States Supreme Court has reversed previous decisions that upheld the white primary, and has subsequently struck down one after another of the attempts that have been made by Southern states to circumvent the court's decision. Recognizing the primary as the real election in the South, the court has refused to uphold party rules excluding the Negro on the grounds that the delegation of this authority by the state 'may make the party's action the action of the State.'

As so frequently happens in this New Reconstruction, a Southern man played one of the key roles in inaugurating the new era. In 1947, Federal District Judge J. Waties Waring of South Carolina was called upon to pass on a new scheme for evading the court's white primary decision, a scheme that had been imitated by Georgia and was being considered by other states. In response to a defiant message from the governor calling for action 'to maintain

125

white supremacy in our Democratic Primaries,' the legislature of South Carolina repealed all laws pertaining to primaries, 150 of them, in an effort to reduce the status of the Democratic party to that of a 'private club.' Judge Waring threw out this scheme as a patent evasion, and the Supreme Court refused to review the case. Still undaunted, the state convention of the Democratic party devised an oath to be required of all voters to the effect that they would support segregation. This time Judge Waring used some of the sternest words one South Carolinian ever delivered from the bench to other South Carolinians: 'It is important that once and for all, the members of this Party be made to understand — and that is the purpose of this opinion — that they will be required to obey and carry out the orders of this court, not only in the technical respects but in the true spirit and meaning of the same.'

Subsequent Supreme Court decisions, including one in 1953, have struck down attempts at evasion, including the 'Boswell Amendment' of Alabama and the so-called 'Jaybird' or three-step scheme of Texas. As a result of these decisions and of other forces, the Negroes have been returning to the polls of the South in large numbers. A study sponsored by the Southern Regional Council indicates that in 1940 only about 2 per cent of the total number of Negroes of voting age in twelve Southern states qualified to vote, but that by 1947 some 12 per cent,

126

or more than 600,000 were so qualified. The number of registered Negro voters in those states increased to 750,000 by 1948, and to 1,200,000 in 1952, and was still growing rapidly. Other estimates place these figures higher than those quoted above. The most sensational increase in the number of Negro registrants was in Louisiana, where the number jumped from 1,672 in 1948 to 108,724 in 1952 — an interesting reversal of the results of disfranchisement and the poll tax in Louisiana, whereby the number fell from 130,334 in 1896 to 1,342 in 1904. According to estimates made by the Southern Regional Council (or the exact figure where available), the Negro registration of 1952 in the other Southern states was 50,000 in Alabama, 65,000 in Arkansas, 120,913 in Florida, 144,835 in Georgia, 20,000 in Mississippi, 100,000 in North Carolina, 60,000 in Oklahoma, 85,000 in Tennessee, 175,000 in Texas, and 70,000 in Virginia.

The violence and unrest that had been expected to result from the return of the Negro to the voting places have simply not materialized. Instead he has been quietly reintegrated in the electorate and has occupied an increasingly significant place in the political community. In the years 1951–1954 Negroes have been appointed or elected to the city school boards of Richmond, Roanoke, Newport News, and Lynchburg, Virginia; Atlanta and Augusta, Georgia; Knoxville and Nashville, Tennessee; San Antonio, Texas; Darlington, South Carolina; and Raleigh, North Carolina. In the years 1952–1954 Negroes have served on the state boards of education in Maryland, Kentucky, and North Carolina. Negroes have secured places on the city councils of Richmond, Greensboro, Winston-Salem, and Nashville. According to George Mitchell of the Southern Regional Council, 'Sixteen major Southern cities [in 1953] employ nearly 65,000 Negro persons, and 468 of these are engaged in managerial or professional tasks.'

Contemporaneous with the appearance of increasing numbers of Negroes on the lists of registered voters has been a marked decline in the readiness of politicians to appeal to race prejudice. It may be of some significance that the anti-Negro propaganda that was used so effectively to elect Willis Smith and defeat Frank Graham for the Senate in North Carolina in 1950 failed of its purpose when the same tactics were revived against Kerr Scott in his race for governor in 1954. While the facts are too few and the time has been too short to establish a trend, it would seem that with the disappearance of such figures as Theodore Bilbo, John E. Rankin, and Eugene Cox over the last few years, and the simultaneous appearance of certain figures in the Middle West, there might have been a slight geographical shift in the center of the demagogue belt.

128

In their struggle for justice in the courts, as in
their fight for the ballot, the Negroes have been
greatly aided by a friendly Supreme Court. In a
series of decisions, beginning in 1939, the court has
repeatedly ordered new trials for Negro defendants
on the ground that members of their race had been
systematically excluded from jury service in the
counties where the trial took place. As a consequence Negroes have been on both juries and grand
juries in increasing numbers during the last few
years. The effort of the civil-rights groups to secure
passage of a federal anti-lynching law have failed,
but the quieter and no less devoted work of religious
and nonsectarian organizations, as well as the courage of some local Southern law-enforcement officials, have all but removed this public disgrace.
No death from lynching has occurred in recent
years. Even the N.A.A.C.P. concedes that 'the virtual disappearance of this form of oppression had
been so well established that lynching is no longer
regarded as an index to the state of intergroup relations.'

Segregation in universities, colleges, and schools
has long been regarded by the Negroes and their
pressure groups as one of the major impediments to
equality of opportunity. They have relied in their
fight against segregation in this field upon the 'equal
protection' clause of the Fourteenth Amendment,
and their effort has been to overturn the 'separate but

129

equal' doctrine laid down in 1896 in the *Plessy* v. *Ferguson* case. The Supreme Court has responded with several decisions that have increasingly broadened the definition of 'equality' and increasingly found 'separation' incompatible with it. A Missouri case in 1938 and an Oklahoma case in 1948, both involving Negro admission to a state school, indicated that the court would insist upon the provision of equal training opportunities, regardless of how few Negroes applied for them. But two cases in 1950 cracked the wall of segregation in higher education. In *Sweatt* v. *Painter*, a Texas case, the court ruled that a hastily established law school for Negroes did not meet the standard of equality because of 'those qualities which are incapable of objective measurement but which make for the greatness in a law school.' On the same day, in *McLaurin* v. *Oklahoma*, the court ruled that even though a graduate student was admitted to the University of Oklahoma for instruction, he did not enjoy the equality guaranteed by the Fourteenth Amendment so long as he was segregated within the classroom, the cafeteria, and the library. 'Such restrictions,' held the court, 'impair and inhibit his ability to study, engage in discussions and exchange views with other students, and, in general, to learn his profession.' That decision would seem to have practically outlawed segregation in higher education.

And so for the first time, except for abortive and

130

ill-prepared attempts in the First Reconstruction, Negro students began to appear on the white campus — even where it was called a 'Lawn.' The first one admitted to the law school of the University of Arkansas was given instruction in a basement during the first month of his attendance. He was then moved up to the regular classroom but placed at a desk in the corner surrounded by a railing. The railing was soon removed, and the second year he sat with two more Negro students on the front row. During the third year the Negroes were permitted to sit anywhere. At the University of Oklahoma the Negro graduate student whose case went to the Supreme Court was first seated in a room adjoining the classroom, and given a separate table in the library and in the cafeteria, but was eventually accepted on an equal basis.

No violence and no serious resistance were reported to have come from the campuses involved before the end of 1955. On the other hand, the opinion of college students seems to have been considerably in advance of that of their elders. A student paper of the University of Mississippi asked for 'admission of Negroes to white graduate schools' and held that 'the pigment of a man's skin should not make any difference.' These views were supported by student papers at Auburn Institute, Millsaps College, and Emory University. The Florida State Student Government Association passed a resolu-

131

tion in 1951 opposing segregation, though the Executive Council of the University of Florida student body then voted to drop out of the state association. When the University of North Carolina refused to permit newly admitted Negro students to sit in the cheering section at football games, the ruling was criticized by fourteen student organizations on the campus and was promptly rescinded by administration authorities. In November 1953, the weekly student paper of the University of Georgia carried an editorial taking a liberal position on segregation and criticizing Governor Talmadge's position. A university trustee and Talmadge supporter denounced the paper and the university placed it under censorship. Whereupon the editor and managing editor resigned, and when censorship continued their successors also resigned. Several informal polls of student and faculty opinion have registered majorities against segregation. The University of Texas student publication commended the Supreme Court decision in *Sweatt* v. *Painter* ordering the admission of a Negro to the law school. The editor declared that 'All over the South the new change is being accepted with good grace. Nowhere has there been a suggestion that race relations have been injured, rather to the contrary.'

Faculty opinion in Southern colleges and universities, somewhat less articulate, has tended to support student opinion. Of the 3,375 Southern college

132

teachers who responded to a poll taken by the Southern Conference Educational Fund in 1949, 70 per cent favored admission of Negroes to professional and graduate schools in the South on a nonsegregated basis, and 25 per cent favored the regional graduate-school plan for the Negroes. The latter reference is to the Southern Regional Education plan, which had been concerned with numerous problems of higher education in the South, but had been erroneously regarded as a means of perpetuating segregation in state graduate facilities. The plan was suspected by some of attempting to assign separate Negro and white graduate and professional schools to which member states might send their students. When the state of Maryland attempted to send a student to a Negro medical school in Tennessee for a course in nursing, the highest Maryland court put a stop to the plan and ordered the University of Maryland to admit the applicant. The United States Supreme Court allowed the Maryland court decision to stand, thus apparently thwarting any segregation designs which this particular case may have embodied.

Among private Southern institutions for professional training, theological schools have been foremost in taking the initiative against segregation. In some schools — for example, Sewanee — this has not been done without resistance. In June 1952, the Board of Trustees of the School of Theology at

Sewanee rejected the request of the Fourth Provincial Synod of the Episcopal Church to admit students without regard for race. The University of the South, of which the Theology School is a part, is owned and operated by the twenty-two Episcopal dioceses governing all the Southern states. The dean and eight faculty members of the theological school requested their trustees to reconsider the action against racial exclusion and declared they would resign if the petition were refused. The following October their resignations were accepted, effective at the end of the school year. Whereupon thirteen Southern bishops of the Episcopal Church met and requested the Chancellor of the University to call a meeting to discuss the issue. In June 1953, the Board of Trustees adopted by a large majority a resolution instructing the administration 'to consider all applications for admission to the School of Theology on the same basis regardless of race.'

By the fall of 1953 Negroes had been admitted to publicly maintained graduate or professional schools in all states except Alabama, Florida, Georgia, Mississippi, and South Carolina. The University of North Carolina had admitted two Negro students at the undergraduate level because they could not get courses they wanted at the Negro college. Louisiana State University had admitted one Negro undergraduate pending litigation, but later canceled his registration. Negroes had also been ad-

134

mitted at the undergraduate level to Virginia Poly-
technic Institution, to a junior college in Paducah,
Kentucky, and to four junior colleges in Texas. As
of September 1953, Negroes were enrolled in
twenty-three state-supported schools of the graduate
or professional level in Southern or border states,
and in ten state or municipal supported schools at
the undergraduate level. In four years an estimated
2000 Negroes had been enrolled on regular terms
at publicly supported Southern schools that had
hitherto been on a segregated basis. This does not
include predominantly Negro schools that admitted
some white students. Privately maintained institutions were falling in line more rapidly, for by the
same date forty-three such colleges and universities
in Southern and border states had enrolled some
Negroes.

Field studies on seventeen of the racially integrated campuses of the South, directed by Professor
Guy B. Johnson in the summer of 1953, indicated
a peaceful adjustment to the new pattern. 'In almost every instance,' writes Professor Johnson,
'when a state institution was faced with the fact that
it might actually have to admit Negroes, there were
serious predictions of violence and bloodshed *if*
this thing came to pass. To the best of our knowl-
edge, the first drop of blood is yet to be shed.'

Far more Southerners than those involved in
higher education were directly affected by the blow

at segregation that has revolutionized American military policy and ended the ancient rule of Jim Crow in the armed services. This revolution was accomplished not by the courts or by Congress but by executive decision and military order from superior to subordinate, without very much discussion or debate save at the higher levels. Trained in the old regime, the generals and colonels, the admirals and captains who carried the new policy into effect were often convinced that it would not work, but orders are orders. Fearful of public reaction, the military succeeded for the most part in keeping out of the press any news of the swift transformation they were working. Both Southern and Northern congressmen entered the conspiracy of silence, so that the full import of the new policy did not become generally known until the end of 1953. By that time desegregation was virtually a *fait accompli* throughout all branches of the armed service, and there was no turning back. Here was 'military reconstruction' with a vengeance — not in the old sense of an occupation of the South, but turned in upon itself.

During the Second World War a few minor cracks had been made in the military wall of segregation. Officer-candidate schools of the army were run without regard for race, and some experiments were conducted in placing Negro platoons in white combat companies. But at the end of the war the

136

old system was almost completely intact. In 1946, however, the navy, which had segregated the great mass of its Negro personnel in the messman's corps, began integration of the races. The newly reorganized air force inaugurated the policy soon afterward. With a greater number and a larger proportion of Negroes than any other branch, the army showed much more resistance to the idea. Then on 26 July 1948, President Truman issued an executive order 'that there shall be equality of treatment and opportunity for all persons in the armed services without regard to race, color, religion or national origin.' At the same time he appointed Charles Fahy, who was born and reared in Georgia, as chairman of a Committee on Equality of Treatment and Opportunity in the Armed Services, with a view 'to carrying out the policy of this order.' In May 1950, the committee reported that in the navy, 'Negroes in general service are completely integrated with whites in basic training, technical schools, on the job, in messes and sleeping quarters, ashore and afloat.' The air force had integrated about three-fourths of all Negroes in 1,301 mixed Negro-white units and had opened up all its schools and jobs to both races without discrimination. The army lagged behind until the crisis of the Korean war, which began in the summer of 1950. With a surplus of Negro troops piling up behind the lines and a critical shortage of white troops, who were bearing the brunt of casualties, one regimental commander in Korea explained that the 'force of circumstances' compelled him to integrate surplus Negroes into his decimated white platoons. It worked. Platoon leaders were delighted to have them. Men in the ranks accepted them. The Negroes fought better than they had before. Race relations took a turn for the better instead of for the worse as feared. General Matthew R. Ridgway asked and was granted permission to integrate Negroes throughout his Korean command.

Tested under fire, the new policy was rapidly applied to occupation and garrison troops in Austria, Germany, Japan, and throughout the many lands and continents in which American troops were stationed. With a rigor suggestive of Cromwellian 'thorough,' the integration policy was also pushed forward at home. It was applied with no diminution or concession in the great army training camps in the Carolinas and Georgia, at the air bases in Alabama and Texas, at the naval bases in Virginia and Florida. It involved Negroes giving orders to whites, as well as whites to Negroes. It was extended to civilian employees as well as enlisted personnel, to living quarters of officers' families as well as to schools for their children. It did not stop at sleeping and eating arrangements, at bars, clubs, athletic fields, or swimming pools. 'Thorough' was the word, and it was passed on. Orders are orders to corporals as well as to colonels. For the full impact of the results one needs the picture supplied by Lee Nichols of a company barracks at Fort Jackson, South Carolina, where, 'busily cleaning their rifles, Negroes from Mississippi and Arkansas sat on double-decker bunks among whites from Georgia and South Carolina with no apparent antipathy.'

One may or may not agree with Harry Truman that racial integration in the armed services is 'the greatest thing that ever happened to America.' But agree or not, there it is.

Extensive studies have been made by the military as well as by independent social scientists to assess the results of integration. Inconclusive though they may be, these studies indicate no substantiation for the old prediction of deterioration of military efficiency or of racial relations. They suggest instead increased efficiency and improved relations. Studies also indicate the Southern states do not differ appreciably from Northern and border states in absorbing and adjusting to these radical changes.

The long-range significance of the new military policy extends far beyond the limits of the armed services. Under the selective-service laws hundreds of thousands of young people pour into one or another of the service branches every year. We seem to be approaching the point where almost every able-bodied male is subject to call. Every year hundreds of thousands of these men are discharged and reenter civilian life. They are on the average about two years older, but that is not the only difference. They have lived those two years under a set of circumstances that very few of them, whether Northerners or Southerners, would have ever duplicated otherwise. It will be a long time before we can know how far and in how many subtle ways and directions the military experience of unsegregated life will carry over into civilian life. But that its impact will be felt can hardly be doubted.

5

TO EXPLORE all the ramifications of the New Reconstruction would be to attempt a superficial sociological survey of the whole South. A mere sampling is all that is within the range of this essay. Because of its historic interest as one of the earliest areas in which the Jim Crow lawmakers entered and because the Jim Crow car became the very symbol of the system, transportation deserves at least passing notice. Here it is the familiar story of a Supreme Court that has gradually sharpened its insistence upon equality of accommodations in 'separate but equal' facilities, and then eventually ruled out segregation itself. The decisions have been concerned with carriers engaged in interstate, not intrastate, commerce. Not until 1946 did the court, in *Morgan* v. *Virginia,* throw out a state law requiring segregation of a carrier, in this case a bus, crossing state

140

lines. Four years later the court ruled against a railway company's practice of segregating Negroes on diners. The main effect of such decisions has been confined to Pullman cars and dining cars. The Jim Crow day coach, in which the mass of the Negroes travel anyway, is still a conspicuous feature of railway landscape. A few of the larger carriers, however, notably the Pennsylvania Railroad and the Southern Railway Company, have discontinued segregation on trains going from New York to points south of Washington, D.C. In intrastate transportation the Jim Crow principle remains fairly intact.

President Roosevelt's Committee on Fair Employment Practices set up in 1941, combined with the wartime shortage of manpower, effected some progress in eliminating race discrimination in federal employment and in the employment practices of some private firms. The effort to enact a permanent federal law embodying the same principles met with failure, however, and discrimination remained the rule. A few large industries in the South have announced that they would open job opportunities without regard for race, and the larger labor organizations have been opening their ranks to include Negroes as members. A study of employment conditions in the upper South made by resident Southerners for the National Planning Association and published in 1953, however, indicates that in spite

141

of some new openings for Negroes the color line in employment has not altered very much in the last fifteen years.

Residential segregation in the cities, buttressed by thousands of supporters from vested interest beyond the reach of laws and courts, has yielded but little to the movement against discrimination. Perhaps the most significant gain registered has been the Supreme Court decision of 1948 that held invalid the judicial enforcement of private restrictive covenants on the ground that they deprived minorities of their right to the equal protection of the laws. The spread of public housing and the increased participation of the federal government in the financing and regulation of housing development have had some effect upon segregation barriers. But, on the whole, residential separation of the races is the prevailing principle.

So far in this narrative the impression has probably been left that the South has retreated on the Jim Crow principle only before the wrath of a stern Supreme Court, a determined President, or an army general brandishing military orders. To leave that impression would be both unfair to the South and unfaithful to the facts. Slow, patient, devoted work of many Southerners of both races has laid the foundation of a new order. The successful Southern campaign against lynching has already been recounted. The Southern Regional Council has reported marked improvement in treatment of Negro news by Southern newspapers. Six states of the South have passed laws aimed at the Ku Klux Klan and prohibiting the wearing of masks and burning of crosses in public places. The forty-odd private universities and colleges that have admitted Negro students have done so without legal compulsion. Southern collegiate teams, the first of which was the University of Virginia, have begun to play Northern teams with Negro members. Negroes have played on professional baseball teams in Florida, Louisiana, North Carolina, Oklahoma, and Texas, and on four teams of the Piedmont League in Virginia. Several Southern cities have opened their public libraries, museums, and parks on a non-segregated basis. Negro artists, entertainers, and speakers have repeatedly appeared before unsegregated audiences.

Private organizations and associations, beyond the reach of the law in this respect, have voluntarily abandoned the color line. Church-affiliated activities, Protestant and Catholic, have often taken the lead. Twelve hospitals in Southern and border states have added Negro doctors to their staffs. Academic associations of the various branches of learning have for some years admitted Negro members and made efforts to accommodate them at their meetings. By 1950, of the other professional associations in the South, lawyers were admitted in six

143

states, doctors in one, nurses in eight, librarians in six, and social workers in all. Several others have opened their doors since 1950. In 1953 the trend toward unrestricted membership in private organizations reached some sort of climax when the Grand Dragon of the Florida Ku Klux Klan announced that Negroes were eligible for membership. They would be required, however, to remain in Jim Crow 'Klaverns.'

In the meantime, the Southern states were finding it harder and harder to meet the ever-stiffening standards of 'equality' the Supreme Court was applying in cases involving public primary and secondary schools. For the court was not only raising its standard but also acting in a supervisory way to enforce its orders. It became increasingly apparent from the court's equalization orders and its close scrutiny of results that if the public schools were to remain 'separate but equal,' they would have to be equal in fact as well as in theory. They were a long way from that in almost all respects. Seeing the handwriting on the wall and realizing that if they did not achieve real equality soon the court would put an end to segregation entirely, several states — especially those with the largest proportion of Negroes — began a dash for equalization in the late 'forties.

Given the distance they had to go and the handicaps under which they had to work, their chances were slight from the start. Even with the huge exodus of Negroes, the proportion of Negro children going to school and the length of time they were attending were constantly increasing because of improvements in Negro family income and decline in Negro infant mortality. The average daily attendance of public schools swelled enormously in the 'forties. Unprecedented appropriations were passed and bond issues authorized, not only to keep up with the increased demand but also to hasten equalization. The thirteen Southern states spent nearly four times as much for school operations in 1951–2 as they had in 1939–40, and about eight times as much for school construction and maintenance. A disproportionate amount of this money was assigned to the Negro schools.

Acknowledging that time was running out and that correction of disparities in the dual educational system was long overdue, Governor Byrnes of South Carolina admitted that 'To meet this situation we are forced to do now what we should have been doing for the last fifty years.' The question was whether the neglect and injustice of fifty years could be repaired before the courts would close forever the separate-but-equal loophole for segregated schools. With emergency appropriations and heroic measures the South began to narrow the gap between Negro and white schools. The gap was very nearly closed in the pupil-teacher ratio, in the

145

length of the school terms, in the amount of teacher training, and appreciably shortened in teachers' pay. But in spite of pressure and strain put into the effort, the differential between white and Negro education yawned wide in many areas. The Supreme Court, moreover, was in the meantime continually enlarging the task set for the South by widening the standards of equality to include such factors as appearance of buildings, the number of toilets, drinking fountains, athletic facilities, courses in the curriculum, and the distance to the school and conditions of roads.

This was not the South's only educational problem. The burden of equalizing white and Negro schools was secondary in expense to the additional burdens of an increasing school population, the equalization of rural and urban standards, and a modest effort to diminish the great gap between Southern and national standards. According to the recent study directed by Harry S. Ashmore, if the South undertook to meet all these needs by 1962, it would have to pay a school bill by that year of about $2,500,000,000, which would be an increase of more than 50 per cent over the bill for 1951–2. Even then the South's general average would lag behind that of many non-Southern states in 1951. The South would have to do that on the lowest per-capita income in the country and by continuing to spend a larger proportion of that income for education than any other region spends. The South would also have to make the unwarranted assumption that its income was going to continue to increase for the next several years at the rate it has been increasing during the boom period. In addition to these very real financial discouragements to the struggle for equalization of racial disparities in public schools, there was the growing realization — privately admitted by some Southern political and educational leaders — that segregation would be gone with the wind anyway, sooner or later, whatever the budget figures showed and whatever the courts decided in current litigation.

The Supreme Court had in the meantime been moving cautiously and deliberately toward a momentous decision. Five cases challenging the principle of segregation in schools had been moving slowly up from South Carolina, Virginia, Delaware, Kansas, and Washington, D.C. Represented by attorneys for the N.A.A.C.P. in all but one case, the plaintiffs were attacking not merely inequality but segregation itself. Here was a concerted challenge to the doctrine of separate but equal laid down in the *Plessy* case in 1896. The court held one hearing in December of 1952 and then ordered the litigants to submit briefs on an elaborate list of questions for a new hearing that was held a year after the first. All arguments were having their day in court, and all points of view were heard. Tempers had time to

147

cool somewhat as the decision was awaited. 'Of only one thing can we be certain,' declared Governor Byrnes, a former associate justice of the Supreme Court. 'South Carolina will not now, nor for some years to come, mix white and colored children in our schools.' But the governor did not say how many years the event would be postponed, even though he threatened to abandon the public-school system.

On 17 May 1954, the court handed down a unanimous decision in favor of the Negro plaintiffs. Dismissing historical argument regarding the intention of the Fourteenth Amendment toward the schools as inconclusive, and citing psychological and sociological authorities, the decision held that 'Segregation of white and colored children in public schools has a detrimental effect upon the colored children,' that 'in the field of public education the doctrine of separate but equal has no place,' and that 'Separate educational facilities are inherently unequal.' The plaintiffs had therefore been 'deprived of the equal protection of the laws guaranteed by the Fourteenth Amendment,' and consequently segregation was unconstitutional.

Southern press reaction was surprisingly mild. This was no doubt due in part to the court's acknowledgment of the many difficulties that would be involved in doing away with segregation and its evident tolerance of a gradualistic approach toward a solution. It was quite evident that a long transitional period was inevitable. The court's order applied directly to only five out of the 11,173 school districts where segregation has been legal. The possibilities of delaying tactics were large, and it is well known that many things that have been declared unconstitutional have continued to exist for a long time.

All this is not to obscure the fact that the court's decision of 17 May is so far the most momentous and far reaching of the many that have affected race relations in recent years. It goes much deeper into the lives of the people and affects more of them and for a longer time than any previous decision. Potentially it affects more than twelve million school children and their parents, and indirectly all citizens. It bears much more directly on the sensitive area Southerners call 'social equality' than does the mixing of the races at the polls, on the trains, in sports and amusements. A unanimous decision, it has all the moral and legal authority of the Supreme Court behind it, and it is unthinkable that it can be indefinitely evaded.

6

A PREOCCUPATION in these pages with the legal aspects and voluntary instances of the abandonment of segregation might create the impression that segregation is finished in the South. That would certainly be a premature announcement of the demise of Jim Crow. For segregation is still the rule and

149

non-segregation the exception. Let us belatedly give William Graham Sumner his due. Even if he were in error about his inscrutable 'folkways' and their imperviousness to legislation, he was surely right that law is not the whole story. Sometimes law merely registers what has already been sanctioned by custom; sometimes it indicates a frantic effort to lock the barn door after the horse has escaped; and sometimes it registers a disturbed conscience and a pious hope of a remote majority essentially unaffected by the law's demands.

It is quite apparent that segregation has continued to flourish and sometimes to grow in other parts of the country long after the collapse of the whole legal foundation for the system. It has continued even after the enactment of stringent civil rights codes outlawing the system. The so-called 'voluntary' principle by which Negro children 'elect' to go to exclusively Negro schools, or by which their parents choose to stay away from places and privileges and opportunities when they know they are not wanted, suggests the possibilities of non-legal segregation. There is no reason to suppose that what has happened in the North after the legal support of Jim Crow was demolished will not happen also in the South.

In the meantime the South finds itself repeating some phases of a familiar historic pattern. In the era of the first emancipation and the first Recon-

150

struction the South also bore the brunt of what Victor Hugo once called 'an idea whose time has come.' Over the South at that time stood an impatient and critical North, furiously aroused with moral indignation. The North had taken more than half a century of debate and gradualistic abolition to solve a problem that was minor in comparison with its dimensions in the South. Yet the North was demanding that the South solve the problem immediately, without debate or gradualism. In the New Reconstruction there has also been impatience, but there has been a little more time for debate, a little more room for gradualism. Feeling its grievances as it does, and remembering the analogy with the First Reconstruction, the South has on the whole shown more forbearance and restraint than might have been expected.

In its present plight the South might cast a glance back over its shoulder to South Africa, with which it once identified itself and seemed to see eye to eye. Alan Paton, a son of South Africa, has described what he calls the 'tragic dilemma' of the white man in Paton's native land. 'A man is caught on the face of a cliff,' he writes. 'As he sees it, he cannot go up and he cannot go down; if he stays where he is, he will die. All those who stand watching have pity for him. But the analogy, alas, is obviously incomplete, for the world's spectators of our drama are seldom pitiful; they are more often reproachful.

151

From their point of vantage they can see which way we ought to go, but they see us taking some other way which will lead us to destruction. And . . . the world looks at us in astonishment, wondering what madness has possessed us.'

The South no longer identifies herself with South Africa and no longer has reason to fear the madness of self destruction. The South somewhere along the way took a different path. It has joined the spectators who are watching the tragic dilemma of the man on the cliff. But the South will watch with more pity and less reproachfulness than some of the spectators. For the South still has its own dilemmas, and the spectators have expanded to a world audience. The South's dilemmas may no longer be tragic, but they are none the less real, and the spectators are still reproachful.

IV / 'Deliberate Speed' vs. 'Majestic Instancy'

BETWEEN THE WRITING of the preceding chapter and the writing of this a period of two years has passed. Those who have followed the argument up to this point may have been struck at times by a certain disparity between the tone of restrained optimism in these pages and the gloomier tones in which the subject has subsequently come to be discussed. The disparity is to be accounted for by what has happened in the last two years and the change in mood these events have induced. The purpose of the present chapter is to take these events into account and, in so far as it is possible at this early date, to assess their meaning and place them in historic perspective.

153

1

FOR A TIME after the decision of 17 May 1954, there appeared to be considerable grounds for optimism. The court's precedent breaking opinion seemed to destroy all legal foundations for segregation. Yet there were no sensational outbursts of defiance. The restrained tone of the Southern press and Southern leaders was the subject of wide comment and congratulations. The comment of the Nashville *Tennessean* on the day following the decision was not unique: 'It is not going to bring overnight revolution,' said the editorial, 'but the South is and has been for years a land of change. Its people — of both races — have learned to live with change. They can learn to live with this one. Given a reasonable amount of time and understanding, they will.' None of the old-style demagogues of the sort who had commanded several states a few years back were presently on hand to make capital of the issue. Scattered localities in the border states announced their intention to abolish segregation in the schools, and Washington and Baltimore moved ahead toward that objective with exemplary speed. The late Professor Howard W. Odum of the University of North Carolina, an authority on race relations, went so far as to predict that 'the South is likely to surprise itself and the nation and do an excellent job of readjustment.'

In view of the many readjustments the South

154

had already made in race relations over the preceding decade, Professor Odum's prediction did not seem unreasonable at all. Southern white people had adjusted to the return of the Negroes to the polls, to their appearance on juries, school boards, and white-collar jobs, and to their admission to colleges and universities. The whites had 'moved over' to make room for colored Southerners in various professional associations, collegiate and professional athletic teams, in interstate carriers, dining cars, and Pullman cars. Southern white draftees drilled, ate, and shared barracks with Negro draftees in all the military services, and took orders from commissioned and noncommissioned officers of both races. To each successive stage the South had adjusted peacefully, if often grudgingly.

Surveying all these revolutionary changes in established Southern practices, changes few thought they would live to see, men of good will began to entertain hopeful expectations about the future. Already the Second Reconstruction could be claimed to have accomplished more genuine change in some aspects of human relations than the First Reconstruction had done with all its blood and thunder and histrionics. The Jim Crow system still stood, but its foundations had been shaken. Segregation was on the defensive; in some quarters it was in full retreat. If all this had been accomplished without bloodshed, reasoned the op-

155

timists, perhaps a new day had really dawned. Perhaps the South might eventually take the transition to unsegregated public schools in its stride as well.

There followed a year of marking time until the Supreme Court handed down its decree of implementation, which was not to come until May 1955. In the meantime neither side showed its hand fully. There was neither any appreciable progress toward desegregation in the schools, save in the border states, nor did the segregationists yet mobilize for all-out resistance. It was a period of wait-and-see.

A few signs appeared to indicate what was to come. Mississippi came forward in her historic role as leader of reaction in race policy, just as she had in 1875 to overthrow Reconstruction and in 1890 to disfranchise the Negro. The third 'Mississippi Plan' took the form of the Citizens Councils, which were started at Indianola in July 1954 to wage unremitting war in defense of segregation. Balancing these negative developments, however, voices counseling compliance and moderation continued to be lifted in the South, even in parts of the Deep South. On the whole, during the year that followed the original Supreme Court decision on public school segregation there was remarkably little of the hysteria that was to develop in the South later.

156

The spell was not even broken by the Supreme Court's decree of 31 May 1955 implementing the decision against segregated schools. The decree was actually greeted by some in the South with expressions of relief and even hailed as signifying the Court's acquiescence in indefinite postponement of desegregation. Indeed, the Court had set no deadline for compliance. It had referred sympathetically to the 'solution of varied local school problems' which would require time; it placed the responsibility for solving these problems upon local school authorities, and it charged the Federal district courts with the duty of passing upon 'good faith implementation.'

More than anything else, it was the reference to the district judges and 'their proximity to local conditions' that raised the hopes of segregationists. The old four-handed American game between the South, the courts, the Negro, and the Constitution has been going on throughout our history, and the South knew all the moves. For much the greater part of that period, the courts had played into the hands of the South and the game had gone against the Negro. If now the Supreme Court had changed partners, one could still place one's hopes in the district judges, many of whom were natives of the states in which they sat. This hope was most explicitly voiced by Lieutenant Governor Ernest Vandiver of Georgia, who rejoiced that 'they are

157

steeped in the same traditions that I am . . . A "reasonable time" can be construed as one year or two hundred. . . . Thank God we've got good Federal judges.'

While the judges ground out their answer in the months that followed the Supreme Court's decree, the segregationists watched with growing disappointment and dismay. By January 1956, nineteen court decisions involving school segregation cases had been rendered, and in every one of them the lower courts upheld the Supreme Court ruling that enforced segregation was a denial of equal protection of the law. While some of the decisions took a lenient view of the amount of time required to desegregate, others stressed the 'prompt and reasonable start' required by the Supreme Court's directive and set dates for compliance. School segregation laws were toppled in Florida, Arkansas, Tennessee, and Texas. On 15 February, Federal District Judge J. Skelly Wright, New Orleans-born and educated, smashed Louisiana's plan to preserve segregation in schools through state laws. Judge Wright admitted all the terrible difficulties involved in desegregation, as well as the need for 'the utmost patience, understanding, generosity and forbearance' on the part of all. 'But the magnitude of the problem may not nullify the principle,' he declared in a ringing conclusion. 'And that principle is that we are, all of us, freeborn Ameri-

158

cans, with a right to make our way unfettered by sanctions imposed by man because of the work of God.'

On top of these blows from quarters where comfort had been expected, came renewed attacks from within the South — from the Negroes themselves. No longer the familiar, submissive creatures whom white Southerners thought they knew and understood so well, Negroes now realized that they at last had the law and the courts on their side. It could no longer be pretended that they were indifferent to the issue. They were ready to assert their rights more forthrightly than they had for three generations. In the summer of 1955 the N.A.A.C.P. filed petitions for desegregation signed by local Negroes with 170 school boards in seventeen states.

2

SOMETHING VERY MUCH like a panic seized many parts of the South toward the beginning of 1956, a panic bred of insecurity and fear. Race relations deteriorated in many areas, and as both races recoiled, old lines of communication between them snapped or weakened. On the white side, resistance hardened up and down the line, and in places stiffened into bristling defiance. The Citizens Councils movement spread out from Mississippi into Louisiana, Alabama, Texas, Arkansas, Florida, and Georgia. A national official of the organization in

New Orleans claimed a membership of 500,000 members in eleven states. As a result of their activities, signers of desegregation petitions in Mississippi, in Selma, Alabama, and in Orangeburg, South Carolina, were fired from their jobs and refused credit by stores and banks so as to compel them to withdraw their names. Negroes brought to bear economic weapons of their own, most notably in the bus boycott in Montgomery. There were individual cases of violence against N.A.A.C.P. members and at least one murder. On 6 February occurred the first instance of violence in connection with the admission of a Negro student to a formerly all-white college or university — after more than a thousand cases of such admission in the South. This was the riot on the campus of the University of Alabama over the admission of Miss Autherine Lucy.

The long-feared and long-predicted reaction in the South was at last under way and gaining ground rapidly. In the first shock of apprehension, in genuine fear of more explosions in chain reaction, Southern liberals and moderates raised the cry of forbearance, directed toward the North. Further pressure and haste at the moment, they maintained, would leave them no ground on which to stand and would only provoke additional violence that would defeat the purposes of the reformers. The appeal met with wide response among

160

Northern liberals, many of whom called for an easing of the pressure and a slowing down of the campaign against segregation.

The initiative, however, had already passed over to the reaction. Leadership of the reaction was not limited to disreputable hate groups and rural demagogues. The State of Virginia, usually a seat of moderation and conservatism, lent all her great prestige of leadership in historic crises of the South to the side of reaction. It was Senator Harry F. Byrd who called upon the South for 'massive resistance'; and it was the conservative leaders of his state who claimed the right of 'interposition' of state authority against alleged violation of the Constitution by the Supreme Court, and who pointed the way toward the private-school plan as a means of evading the Court's decision and preserving segregation. In the first three months of 1956 the legislatures of five Southern states — Alabama, Georgia, Mississippi, South Carolina, and Virginia — adopted at least forty-two pro-segregation measures, mainly dealing with schools. Many other measures were pending, and by July twelve new segregation bills had been approved by the Louisiana legislature.

Virginia's interposition plan, or some variation of it, was taken over by all six of the states mentioned in the previous paragraph. Alabama was the first actually to apply the fateful words, 'null, void,

161

and of no effect' to the Supreme Court school decision. The resolution was endorsed by a voice vote
in the Senate and an 86-to-4 vote in the House.
Georgia also adopted the 'null and void' approach,
adding a strongly worded declaration that it intended to ignore the Supreme Court decision. Mississippi declared the decision 'unconstitutional and
of no lawful effect,' and created a State Sovereignty
Committee 'to prohibit . . . compliance with the
integration decisions.' Avoiding the word 'nulli-
fication,' South Carolina contented herself with
'condemnation of and protest against the illegal
encroachment of the central government.' The
Louisiana legislature adopted its interposition resolution without a single negative vote in either
house. The North Carolina legislature defeated
interposition but adopted a 'resolution of protest'
against the Supreme Court decision.

In addition to these more or less rhetorical ges-
tures of defiance, four states have bluntly proclaimed a policy of open resistance by imposing
sanctions and penalties against compliance with
the Supreme Court's decision. The Louisiana legislature would withhold approval and funds from
'any school violating the segregation provision' of
its laws. Georgia made it a 'felony for any school
official of the state or any municipal or country
schools to spend tax money for public schools in
which the races are mixed.' North Carolina would

162

also deny funds to local authorities who integrated their schools, and Mississippi made it unlawful for the races to attend publicly supported schools together at the high school level or below. Both Mississippi and Louisiana amended their constitution to provide that to promote public health and morals their schools be operated separately for white and Negro children.

Such undisguised defiance as these measures represent is more significant as a barometer of popular resentment than as an effective legal defense of segregated schools. Probably in the same category, though somewhat more serious as an obstacle to integration, belong the various state plans for evading desegregation by substituting some form of private education for the public schools. These plans are analogous to those by which South Carolina sought to evade the Supreme Court's ruling against the white primary a few years ago by converting the political party into a private organization and claiming the state had no control over its primary elections. This method applied to education will no doubt meet with no more success before the courts than it did as applied to primaries. This did not prevent several states from resorting to the device. Mississippi and South Carolina amended their constitutions to enable their legislatures, counties, or school districts to abolish the public schools, and Georgia

163

entertained a similar amendment. Alabama provided permissive legislation enabling the state and its subdivisions to discontinue public schools and turn over public money to aid private education. Georgia and North Carolina would make grants to parents of school-age children to be used in paying private tuition. These measures were accompanied in some states by various provisions for leasing or selling of school buildings and property to private individuals. It is difficult to take these plans very seriously as solutions for either the constitutional or the educational problems involved, and few of their authors could have expected them to stand the test of the courts very long.

More serious as obstacles to the progress of desegregation were the numerous new regulations governing assignment and attendance of pupils. They were generally designed to create administrative obstacles to legal action and tie up and string out litigation so as to discourage efforts at integration. A key device of this sort was the transfer of all authority over assignment and enrollment of pupils to local authorities. This would make it necessary to sue each local authority individually and thereby slow down the pace of litigation. Appeal from a decision denying a child admission to a school in North Carolina was made difficult, slow, and expensive. The parent had to carry an appeal first to the local board, then to the Superior

164

Court, in which a jury trial was required, and from there an expensive appeal could be made to the state Supreme Court. In framing the new rules governing assignment of pupils, the law makers invoked the police power of the state 'to preserve the peace, protect the health, and morals . . . and insure the peace, health, contentment, happiness, and tranquility to all the people of the state,' as Tennessee put it. Virginia would take into account 'personality, practices, needs and desires; the intensity of racial feeling'; and Georgia authorized local superintendents to consider sociological and psychological data in assigning pupils.

It is unnecessary to labor the possibilities of resistance, evasion, and delay opened by laws of this sort. 'There is no one way, but many,' as John Temple Graves of Alabama has pointed out. 'The South proposes to use all of them that make for resistance. The decision tortured the Constitution — the South will torture the decision.' The Court ruled against segregation on grounds of race or color only — not against segregation on grounds of health, morals, illegitimate birth, public welfare and tranquility. On grounds comparable to these the Negro was for half a century denied the ballot that the Fifteenth Amendment plainly said he could not be denied on grounds of race or color. And when those possibilities are exhausted, there still remain token compliance accompanied by real

165

evasion and all the devices of 'voluntary' segregation which are effectively and quietly used in other parts of the country without any legal support at all.

As yet there are no 'teeth' in the Court's decision against segregated schools. That is, there are no sanctions such as the Civil Rights Act gave to the Fourteenth Amendment for a time during Reconstruction, or the Volstead Act gave to the Eighteenth Amendment. The only person who can be jailed for disobedience is the official who refuses to execute an order of the court specifically applying to him. State laws can gradually be brought to test before the courts. But there are thousands of local school boards in the segregating states to which the ball can be passed by the state, and they in turn can invent new troubles for the courts.

Progress toward desegregation of public schools during the two and a half years that followed the Supreme Court decision was not very impressive, and it was largely confined to the border states and the District of Columbia. The school year 1956–57 opened in the seventeen Southern and border states with 723 school districts and school units desegregated, a gain of 186 over the previous year. Of those districts that had any Negro pupils, some 3,000 remained segregated. In all, approximately 300,000 Negro pupils were in 'integrated situations,' though not necessarily going to school with whites, and about 2,400,000 were entirely segregated. Two schools in Tennessee, three school districts in Arkansas, and more than a hundred school districts in western Texas were desegregated. But in the eight states of Alabama, Florida, Georgia, Louisiana, Mississippi, North Carolina, South Carolina, and Virginia the rule of segregation in the lower school level remained unbroken.

For a time it seemed as if the policy of defiance or determined resistance would be followed by only five or six states. The border states gave early indication of compliance, and the so-called mid-South states — Tennessee, Arkansas, Texas, and Florida — appeared to be inclining toward the example of the border states rather than in the opposite direction. From the first, however, heavy pressure was brought to bear upon moderates or waverers to line up with resistance. Proponents of the Southern 'Declaration of Constitutional Principles,' issued on 12 March 1956, were able to get the signatures of all the congressmen from seven states, and 101 of the 128 members from eleven states. Among the signers were several political leaders who had previously spoken in tones of moderation and from whom better leadership was expected. Yet the manifesto deplored the Supreme Court's 'clear abuse of judicial powers' and commended 'the motives of those states which have declared the intention to resist forced integration by any lawful means.'

In the spring of 1956 the school segregation issue figured prominently in seven state primary elections. Two North Carolina congressmen who refused to sign the Southern manifesto against the Supreme Court went down to defeat. Governor James E. Folsom of Alabama became a major casualty of the segregation issue by losing almost three-to-one to a pro-segregationist in a race for election as Democratic national committeeman. The policy of resistance spread southward into Florida, westward into Arkansas, and northward into Tennessee. Under the leadership of Governor LeRoy Collins, Florida had professed an official policy of gradual acceptance of integration. In March 1956, however, Governor Collins declared that 'we are just as determined as any Southern state to maintain segregation.' In the same month Governor Orval Faubus of Arkansas, where there had already been a small start at integration, took a stand for segregation that won the praise of the executive secretary of White America, Inc. The governors of North Carolina and Texas announced strong support for new segregation laws in their states. During the summer of 1956 the legislatures of Florida, North Carolina, and Virginia were called into special sessions to consider bills de-

168

signed to tighten segregation laws. When the schools opened in the fall, flurries of violence broke out in Tennessee, Texas, Kentucky, and West Virginia as mobs sought to block the admission of Negro pupils to newly desegregated schools.

There is little doubt but that some of this defiance can be discounted as the bluster of political expediency in an election year. On the other hand, it would be a grave mistake to dismiss the whole resistance movement in this fashion. Much of it was deeply felt and in deadly earnest. However hollow and antiquated the constitutional arguments may seem to others, they were self-evident truths to a great many people in the South. This was a real constitutional crisis that the country was facing. The law of the land had been clearly defined by the Supreme Court of the United States, and that definition had been just as clearly rejected by responsible spokesmen of millions of our people.

3

IN THE FACE of these discouraging developments, there is little wonder that the optimism of 1954 had given way before a more pessimistic outlook. In this mood and in view of prevailing retrogression, it is natural to speculate whether the New Reconstruction, in spite of its promising start, is not doomed to repeat the frustration and failure of the First Reconstruction.

169

A comparison between the two periods of reconstruction would not, on the face of it, offer much encouragement about the prospects of the current experiment. After all, in the 1860's the South was conquered territory under military occupation, virtually helpless before the will of the conqueror. Its leaders and many of its voters were disfranchised. As for its representatives, they were not even admitted to Congress, much less consulted about their views, until the revolutionary changes in the law were accomplished and a newly created electorate had sent representatives to Washington which accepted them. The revolutionary architects of the First Reconstruction, moreover, were untroubled with scruples about state rights and quite ready to use force without stint to accomplish their purposes. If the Constitution got in their way they changed it or ignored it, and they took much the same attitude toward the President and the Supreme Court.

And yet in spite of the relative weakness of the South, in spite of the determined zeal of the Northern reformers, their disregard of constitutional restraints, and their readiness to override opposition and employ coercive force, the fact is that the great experiment ended in disillusionment and default. The initial zeal and idealism of the reformers gave way to apathy and defeatism. In the end it was the will of the defeated, discredited,

170

and, for a time, helpless South that prevailed.

This being the outcome of the First Reconstruction, what can be said of the outlook for the Second? In the second instance the resistance was by no means helpless. Far from being disfranchised, it had more than a hundred representatives in Congress who were capable of being mobilized to combat desegregation. It had a powerful voice in one of the major political parties, and could no longer be ignored by the other. In 1956 the timorous way in which the national nominating conventions of both the Democratic and the Republican parties approached the issue of public school desegregation, the gingerly way in which it was discussed, and the weak and noncommittal planks in the party platforms were all significant indications of the political power of the resistance. The reformers, on the other hand, were divided in council, restrained by constitutional scruples, and reluctant, most of them, to resort to coercion and force. Gradualism, defined by the Supreme Court as 'deliberate speed,' was the approved approach, and the Court had left the responsibility of planning and initiating the desegregation procedures to the local school authorities.

It is true that the present Court has consistently held against segregation. But Americans have developed over the years a curious usage of the law as an appeasement of moralists and reformers.

171

Given sufficient pressure for a law that embodies reputable and popular moral values, the electorate will go to great lengths to gratify the reformers. They will even go so far as to unlimber the cumbersome machinery of Constitutional amendment. But having done this much, they are inclined to regard it as rather tedious of the reformers to insist upon literal enforcement. Under these circumstances the new law is likely to become the subject of pious reference, more honored in the breach than in the observance, a proof of excellent intentions rather than the means of fulfilling them. Much of the history of the Fourteenth, Fifteenth, and Eighteenth Amendments illustrates this usage. It is not at all inconceivable that the new interpretation of the Fourteenth Amendment advanced in the school segregation decision will provide another illustration.

There is still another reflection upon the historical context of the two reconstruction periods that should be taken into account. We are told that the present political temper of the country represents a revolt of the moderates. Moderate or not, there is certainly impressive evidence of popular revulsion from social and economic reform and a widespread swing to conservatism. The electorate has made it evident in many ways that it has had enough, for the time being, of crusading reformers and government interference with private affairs, that it yearns for political tranquility and uninterrupted opportunity to enjoy the blessings of prosperity.

This mood is national, not sectional, and it is as prevalent in the South as in any other part of the country. The only area of affairs in which the government has dared seriously to challenge the prevailing mood and to demand reform and change as drastic as any demanded in the New Deal era (if not more so) is the area of race relations. This gives the exception a geographic boundary as well, for to all practical purposes it singles out the South as the one part of the country in which drastic reform is demanded in an anti-reform era. In this respect the present experiment in reconstruction is not unlike the former one. For the national background of the First Reconstruction was the Gilded Age. It also was a postwar era that, after a few years of peace, had had enough of idealism, self-sacrifice, and crusades and was exuberantly preoccupied in material things and self-indulgence. Normally cynical about politics and incredibly lax in public morality, political leaders of the Gilded Age nevertheless plunged the South into a stiff regimen of revolutionary changes on a heroic scale, aimed at the achievement of idealistic goals. In both eras the reforming impulse, thwarted and baffled elsewhere, found vicarious outlet in the South. And in both periods one finds zealous ad-

173

vocates of reform for the South who in all other respects were entirely in accord with the national temper of complacency and conservatism. Difficult enough to achieve under ideal circumstances, the types of reforms that the two experiments in reconstruction demanded of the South were specially handicapped by the laxity of the national background against which they were attempted, and by the South's natural insistence upon sharing the national resistance to agitation and change.

4

SO FAR, all comparisons drawn between the nineteenth- and twentieth-century experiments in reconstruction have tended to darken the prospects of the current effort and support the more pessimistic outlook. But there are other comparisons to be taken into account.

Reconstruction in the 1860's and '70's was pretty strictly identified in origin, implementation, and execution with the Republican party, and about as consistently opposed by the Democratic party. It was quite clear that, whatever the merits of the reconstruction plan in terms of justice, principle, and human rights, its success spelled political advantage for one party and disadvantage for the other. The creation of a large new electorate devoted to the Republicans and the simultaneous crippling of an electorate equally devoted to the Democrats was one meaning of Reconstruction, the crude political meaning. The Second Reconstruction has no such strongly marked partisan character. It originated under the leadership of one party and was continued by the other. It has received important contributions and encouragement from both. While partisan gains are to be derived from any movement affecting the vital interests of so large a number of people, and while such advantages are constantly sought by politicians, the success of the Second Reconstruction is not tied to the fortunes of one political party. The movement cannot be cynically discredited as political machinations of partisan maneuver. It has sources of strength independent of either party and is respected and feared by politicians for that reason, if for no other.

Negroes played important roles in both reconstruction periods, but it is obvious that in the present movement they are vastly better equipped to defend themselves and advance their cause than were their newly emancipated, propertyless, and largely illiterate grandfathers and great-grandfathers. Negroes have already shown new capacities for leadership that have surprised their friends as well as their opponents. In the long run, it may be that their own resources will prove decisive in the contest.

In both periods of reconstruction, the opposition in the South sought to unite white resistance

175

by appealing to race prejudice and demanding white solidarity. The white supremacy campaign after the Civil War was extremely effective in the construction of a 'solid South.' A comparable campaign is being waged at present, and not without considerable success. But there are significant counter-trends within the South today. The most important of these for the long run is a cleavage between generations. While no systematic general study of the subject is available, sample polls in Texas and Florida, and ordinary observation in many quarters, give evidence of a more liberal — or perhaps more indifferent — attitude toward race relations among white Southerners who came of age during and after the Second World War than among their parents.

The First Reconstruction tended to widen instead of close the sectional breach that had opened with the great national church organizations in the ante-bellum struggle over slavery. While the present movement for Negro rights has revealed sectional differences and occasional debates, virtually all of the major denominations, supported by their Southern branches, have in some degree come out against the segregation system. This tendency has placed some prominent Southern churchmen in advance of prevailing sentiment in the region and made some churches an ally of the movement instead of a drag upon its progress.

176

In the current discouragement over the stalemate in public school desegregation, there is a tendency to overlook the important permanent achievements in other fields which may in the end outlast anything accomplished by the highly ephemeral and perishable works of the First Reconstruction. In the field of higher education, the lowering of racial bars has proceeded much more rapidly and smoothly. As of March 1956, for example, 104 of the 208 formerly all-white, publicly supported colleges and universities in the South had opened their doors at some level to Negroes. Several state institutions still resisting at that time subsequently received court orders to admit Negro students, and the prospect of orderly compliance was good. The excitement over the flare-up of violence at the University of Alabama has obscured the fact that this was the only instance of such violence that had occurred on a Southern campus over the admission of a Negro student.

Another contrast between the two reconstruction movements lies in the impact they had upon the border states. In the first instance the effect was to drive the border states into the South's orbit and add their support to the strength of the resistance. Generally speaking, they became more 'Confederate' after the Civil War than they had been during it. Lincoln's masterly diplomacy in detaching them from the seceding states was undone and reversed by the Radical leaders who overthrew his policy. The Second Reconstruction, on the other hand, has had just the opposite effect, for the defection of the border states from the cause of segregation is becoming more and more apparent. The struggle within Delaware, Maryland, West Virginia, Kentucky, Missouri, and Oklahoma is still far from won, but each month brings news of additional retreats along the segregation front. Not one of the congressmen from Kentucky and Oklahoma, the border states most closely identified with the South, signed the Southern manifesto on state rights.

The struggle for the allegiance of the 'mid-South' states, including Tennessee, Arkansas, Texas, and Florida, three of which have accepted some degree of public-school desegregation, is still being waged and the outcome is undecided. As pointed out above, their tendency in the first half of 1956 was to move in the direction of the Lower South rather than toward the border states. The prospect over the years, however, would seem to be for a steady enlargement of the reconstructed areas, a process moving in gradually from the Southern periphery toward the center of resistance.

In spite of resistance and recent setbacks, therefore, the preponderant evidence points to the eventual doom of segregation in American life and the triumph of the Second Reconstruction — *in the*

178

long run. But the 'long run' implies 'gradualism,' and 'gradualism' is a word that has acquired almost as evil associations as the word 'appeasement' once had. Impatience with the word among people who have already waited nearly a hundred years for promised rights is readily understandable. The word is used here not to propose or define a policy, but to characterize a historic phenomenon. Undesirable or not, gradualism is an inescapable fact and a basic characteristic of the New Reconstruction.

Professor Paul A. Freund of the Harvard Law School has pointed out that the Supreme Court's phrase, 'deliberate speed,' is derived from eighteenth-century chancery practice. It was not inspired, as some would seem to think, by the haunting line from Francis Thompson's poem, *The Hound of Heaven:* 'Deliberate speed, majestic instancy.' Those who prefer the more heroic and poetic construction of the court's ruling would do well to ponder the unhappy history of 'majestic instancy' in the First Reconstruction. However deliberate and halting its speed, the Second Reconstruction would seem to promise more enduring results.

Suggested Reading

A MOST HELPFUL synthesis of modern scholarship in the
field is a collaborative work directed by the Swedish
scholar, Gunnar Myrdal, *An American Dilemma: The
Negro Problem and Modern Democracy* (2 vols., 1944).
John Hope Franklin, *From Slavery to Freedom* (1947)
is the best-informed brief history of the Negro. A critical period of Southern history is treated in C. Vann
Woodward, *Origins of the New South, 1877–1913*
(1951).

Of particular importance for their original investi-
gation of special subjects are Vernon L. Wharton, *The
Negro in Mississippi, 1865–1890* (1947), and George B.
Tindall, *South Carolina Negroes, 1877–1900* (1952).
The desertion of Northern liberals, a neglected subject,
is stressed by R. W. Logan, *The Negro in American
Life and Thought: The Nadir, 1877–1901* (1954). Legal
aspects of race relations are treated in Charles S. Man-

gum, Jr., *The Legal Status of the Negro* (1940); Franklin Johnson, *The Development of State Legislation concerning the Free Negro* (1919); Gilbert T. Stephenson, *Race Distinctions in American Law* (1910); and Pauli Murray, *State Laws on Race and Color* (1952). Sociological phases are the subject of Bertram W. Doyle, *The Etiquette of Race Relations in the South* (1937); Arthur F. Raper, *The Tragedy of Lynching* (1933); and E. Franklin Frazier, *The Negro in the United States* (1949). Various works of John Dollard, particularly *Children of Bondage* (with Allison Davis, 1940), are illuminating. A most helpful essay is one by Guion G. Johnson, 'The Ideology of White Supremacy, 1876–1910,' in Fletcher M. Green, *Essays in Southern History, The James Sprunt Studies in History and Political Science,* vol. 31 (1949).

Race factors in politics are astutely examined in V. O. Key, Jr., *Southern Politics in State and Nation* (1949); and there is much of value in Paul Lewinson, *Race, Class, and Party, A History of Negro Suffrage and White Politics in the South* (1932). William A. Mabry, *The Negro in North Carolina Politics since Reconstruction* (1940) is an able work.

A few guides to recent developments, out of a vast number of publications, are recommended. Howard W. Odum, *Race and Rumors of Race* (1944) gives an account of racial tension during the Second World War. Lee Nichols, *The Breakthrough on the Color Front* (1954) outlines the history of desegregation of the American armed services. Harry S. Ashmore, *The Negro and the Schools* (1954) brings the story of the attack upon segregated schools up to the Supreme Court decision of 17 May 1954. Other aspects of the school situation are treated by Truman Pierce, *Bi-*

Racial Education in the Southern States (1955); Ernest W. Swanson and John A. Griffin, *Public Education in the South Today and Tomorrow* (1955); and Robin M. Williams, Jr., and Margaret W. Ryan, *Schools in Transition* (1954). Morroe Berger, *Equality by Statute: Legal Controls over Group Discrimination* (1952) traces the interplay of pressure group, legislative body, and court decision. Able assessments and evaluations of recent developments in desegregation are to be found in Kenneth B. Clark, 'Desegregation: An Appraisal of Evidence,' *The Journal of Social Issues,* vol. IX, No. 4 (1953); *The Negro Yearbook* of *The Journal of Negro Education* for 1954 and 1955; David Loth and Harold Fleming, *Integration North and South* (1956); and Ira De A. Reid (ed.), *Racial Desegregation and Integration,* which is vol. 304 of *The Annals of the American Academy of Political and Social Science* (March 1956). Of inestimable value are the files of the *Southern School News,* published monthly by the Southern Education Reporting Service.

GALAXY BOOKS

HESPERIDES BOOKS